The Treasury of Clean Senior Adult Jokes

Tal D. Bonham
Jack Gulledge

Broadman Press
Nashville, Tennessee

W9-AFN-135

© Copyright 1989 • Broadman Press
All Rights Reserved
4257-36
ISBN: 0-8054-5736-4

Dewey Decimal Classification: 808.87
Subject Heading: JOKES - COLLECTED // ELDERLY
Library of Congress Catalog Number: 88-17526

Printed in the United States of America

Library of Congress Cataloging-in-Publication Data

Bonham, Tal D., 1934-
  The treasury of clean senior adult jokes / Tal D. Bonham,
Jack Gulledge.
    p. cm.
  ISBN 0-8054-5736-4 (pbk.) : $3.50
  1. Aging—Humor. 2. Old age—Humor. 3. Aged—Humor.
I. Gulledge, Jack, 1924-   II. Title.
PN6231.A43B66 1989
818'.5402'08—dc19   88-17526
                                                    CIP

Writing itself is a lot of laughs. And for those of us lucky enough to make a living at it, it's double the fun. For these years of journalistic joy, I owe a special debt of gratitude to two people—Erwin McDonald and Ernest Mosley.

Erwin, long-time editor of *The Arkansas Baptist Newsmagazine,* not only published my first manuscript in the early 1950s, but tutored me by mail.

In the early 1970s Ernest, who at the time was a supervisor at the Baptist Sunday School Board, gave me my first editor's job.

To my dear friends and fellow scribes, Erwin and Ernest, I dedicate these fun pages.

Jack Gulledge

Introductions

What do you call a book aimed primarily at senior adults? I realize that some people just don't like to be called "senior adults." One famous journalist said, "The next person who calls me a senior citizen, I'm going to call him a junior citizen!" A psychologist friend of mine said, "Maybe it doesn't really matter what they call us as long as they smile when they say it."

Well, we're smiling when we say—here's a joke book designed primarily for senior adults. We hope you enjoy it. We've tried to put it together from the biblical perspective that, "A merry heart doeth good like a medicine" (Prov. 17:22). We hope this little book will be good medicine for you and those with whom you share its humor.

Tal D. Bonham

The person who laughs—*lasts*!

No age group enjoys a lasting laugh more than senior adults. It's God's medicine of mirth for difficult times. Someone has likened humor to shock absorbers to help weary pilgrims over the rough roads of daily struggle. Truly a hearty laugh is like a healing ray of hope in a sickroom of despair. But put on a happy face. "Against the assault of laughter," Mark Twain said, "nothing can stand."

Within these pages you'll find our attempt to pass along a healthy dose of mirth. A few of the stories, collected over many years from forgotten sources, are true; others are not. But they're all designed to help senior adults enjoy the lighter side of life. After all, we can't take life too seriously— we're never going to get out of it alive, anyway!

So sit back. Grin. Turn on the old tickle box. Let the medicine of mirth heal the soul and keep life in perspective.

Repeat daily the prayer of Chester Cathedral:

> Give me a sense of humor, Lord;
> Give me the grace to see a joke,
> To get some happiness from life,
> And pass it on to other folk.

Jack Gulledge

Contents

You Know You're About to Become a Senior Adult When. . .

You don't care where your wife goes as long as you don't have to go with her.

You lose your breath opening the telephone directory.

The grandkids come home and tell you what they are studying in history, and you remember studying the same subjects in current-events class.

You become exhausted simply by wrestling with your conscience.

You decide procrastination is the best approach to life, but you never get around to it.

You look forward to a dull evening.

You walk with your head held high because you're trying to get used to your bifocals.

You sit in a rocking chair and you can't get it going.

Your knees buckle but your belt won't.

Dialing long distance wears you out.

"Burning the midnight oil" means staying up past 9 PM.

Your back goes out more than you do.

You sink your teeth into a steak and they stay there.

You bend over to tie your shoes and look around to see if there's something else you can do while you're down there.

Accidents (Mistakes)

I still get nervous when I speak after all these years. It goes with being a minister. It all started about forty years ago when I performed my first wedding. I did okay until I pronounced them husband and wife and waited for the groom to kiss the bride. But he just stood there. Then in a nervous high-pitched tone I blurted out, "It's kisstomary to cuss the bride!"

And he probably has ever since!

The car skidded to an abrupt stop. The first person on the scene screamed, "Look at that awful sight splattered all over the inside of the windshield!"

"Are you badly hurt?" they asked the man in the front seat.

"Nah," the driver replied, "but this pizza is a mess!"

"What should I take, Doctor," gasped the tense patient, "when I'm run down?"

"Try the license number first," replied the bored doctor, "then get the make of the car!"

A telephone directory in a large city accidentally got this ad mixed in with the listing of funeral directors:

"When away, keep in touch by long distance. Phone ahead for reservations. Let them know you're on the way!"

An obituary notice in a newspaper recounted the impressive rites of a funeral service and then noted that "A spectator slipped at the gravesite and broke his leg. The accident cast a cloud of gloom over the whole occasion."

A man came in to the doctor's office and the receptionist asked him what he had. "Shingles," he answered.

She took his name, address, medical insurance information, and told him to take a seat. Fifteen minutes later, another nurse came in and weighed him, took his temperature, and told him to go into the examining room and take off his clothes.

Thirty minutes later, the doctor came in

and asked him what he had. Again, he answered, "Shingles."

"Where?" the doctor probed.

"Outside in the truck," the bewildered man responded. "Where do you want me to unload them?"

"How in the world did you happen to hit that other car?" asked the policeman investigating the accident.

"It was my wife's fault," the man replied. "She fell asleep in the back seat!"

"Now, Mrs. Marsh, this may sting just a little," the doctor said, as he prepared the syringe of antibiotic and stepped forward to administer it.

The patient suddenly screamed in agonizing pain and crumpled to the floor.

The doctor picked her up and exclaimed, "Mrs. Marsh, this is ridiculous. I haven't even injected the needle yet!"

"No, you haven't," wailed the patient, "but you stepped on my ingrown toenail!"

Once the lady principal in my high school announced sternly in assembly, "The superintendent and I have decided to stop necking on the school grounds."

Realizing what she had said, she tried to make amends and added, "No! What I mean is, all this kissing going on under my nose has got to stop!"

Advice

I like to drive, but one day I had a frightening experience. I was out in the country when my car broke down. I got out to take a look under the hood.

Just then an old horse trotted by, said, "Better check the gasoline," and galloped on down the road. I was so frightened I ran to a nearby farmhouse and told the farmer what had happened.

"Was it an old horse with a floppy ear?" he asked.

"Yes! Yes!" I replied.

"Well, then," the farmer drawled, "don't pay no attention to him. He don't know nothin' about cars."

A doctor questioned his patient: "It's strange you haven't been to see me. Why, you haven't been here in years. What other doctors have you been seeing?"

"No doctors," replied the patient, "only my pharmacist."

"Why, goodness, man!" bellowed the

doctor, "are you in your right mind? Why, that druggist isn't medically qualified. You certainly don't listen to him. What crazy and idiotic thing did he tell you?"

"He told me to come see you!" answered the patient.

Never fall in love with a tennis player. To him, love means nothing.

The young bachelor was visiting with his grandfather about his marital status. "I've dated several women and come close to marriage several times. However," he said, "I just haven't been able to find the wife for me."

The grandfather remarked, "You're going to find yourself left out in the cold some day without a wife."

"Aw," said the young bachelor, "there's plenty of fish left in the sea!"

"Yes," pondered the grandfather. "Just remember that after a while the bait is not what it used to be!"

Stop telling everybody else how you feel. Don't give an "organ recital" every time someone asks, "How are you feeling?" It might help you to remember that 80 percent of the people don't care about your problems, and the other 20 percent of the them are glad you have them!

"Today students, we are honored to have in our midst the oldest practicing physician in the country," exclaimed the professor. "Now, doctor, don't you have a few wise words for these medical students?"

After being helped to his feet and pondering a few minutes, the old gentleman gave the following shaky reply: "Always scribble your prescriptions illegibly. . . and write your bills clearly!"

Aging

My wife bought a new line of expensive cosmetics guaranteed to make her look years younger. After a lengthy sitting before the mirror applying the "miracle" products she asked, "Darling, honestly what age would you say I am?"

Looking over her carefully, I replied, "Judging from your skin, twenty; your hair, eighteen; and your figure, twenty-five."

"Oh, you flatterer!" she gushed.

"Hey, wait a minute!" I interrupted. "I haven't added them up yet."

Growing older is merely a matter of feeling your corns rather than feeling your oats.

A devout Christian was taking the aging process a little hard. As he noticed the wrinkles, loose skin, receding gums, and arthritis, his response was, "I'm not going to say that God made a mistake when he created old age; but I'll tell you one thing, when I get to heaven I'm going to talk to Him about it."

An Old-Timer—one who can remember when a "bureau" was a piece of furniture.

"Now, Mrs. Lyons," said the doctor. "You say you have shooting pains in the neck, dizziness, and constant nausea. Now, just for the record, how old are you?"

"I'm going to be thirty-nine on my next birthday," replied the woman.

"Hmmmmm," muttered the doctor. "Got a slight loss of memory too!"

Trim Figures—what some people do when they tell their age.

Question: How is life like a taxi cab?
Answer: The meter just keeps going whether you're going somewhere or just standing still.

Children—a great comfort in old age, and often that which helps you get there sooner.

What's the point in taking speed-reading courses if they don't teach you how to speed-think?

I have to admit to aging, because:
Now that I know my way around, I don't feel like going!
My forehead is getting higher and my energy lower.
My wife powders and I puff!
It takes me longer to rest than it does to get tired.
I'm at the stage where my passion has turned to pensions.
I can still hear temptation whispering, "Why not? Why not?" But my body shouts back, "Why bother! Why bother!"
And when a cute young thing says I'm a "WOW," she means a "worn-out wolf!"

Senior Adult—Reaching the age where you've got to prove that you are just as good as you never were.

You're never too old to learn. . . but that's no reason to keep putting it off.

Wife: "Well, you really know how to flatter a woman. That was a stroke of genius when you told Mrs. Jones that she didn't look a day older than her daughter."

Husband: "Yeah, did you see the look on her face when I said that?"

Wife: "No, I didn't notice. I was too busy watching the expression on her daughter's face!"

A sign posted at a retirement village: "Lord, keep me alive while I'm still living."

The five "B's" of old age—balding, bursitis, bifocals, bulges, and bunions.

"Crossing the Border"

Senescence begins
And middle age ends
The day your descendants
Outnumber your friends.

—Ogden Nash

A comedian asked an elderly lady, "How old are you?"

"Sir," she replied indignantly, "my age is my business!"

"Well," he said, "it looks like you've been in business a long time!"

Old age is when Father Time catches up with Mother Nature.

It's a time when a person gets exhausted just wrestling with his conscience. And our narrow waists and broad minds change places.

It's a time when the sight of a big, round harvest moon reminds us to have the furnace checked.

It's a time when boys consider women charmless, and girls consider men harmless.

It's a time of life when we shun those crowded gatherings where people outnumber the comfortable chairs.

Arguments

"Why haven't you mended the holes in these socks?" the husband demanded.

"You didn't buy that new coat I wanted," replied his wife, "so I figured if you didn't give a wrap, I didn't give a darn!"

"You're over seventy-five years of age, slim and trim, and with a tremendous tan. What's the secret of your success?" asked the doctor.

"Well," he explained, "my wife and I

have been married for over fifty years. Before we got married we agreed that if I ever lost my temper that I was to say nothing."

"That sounds good," said the doctor. "What kind of arrangement did your wife make in case she lost her temper?"

"We agreed that if she ever lost her temper that I would simply go outside. That's where my good health comes in. I've spent most of my life outdoors."

One couple lived together for sixty years without a single argument. Their secret? They shared the same hearing aid!

A man and his wife were eating in a restaurant in Canton, Ohio. They were having an argument on how to pronounce *Canton*. He said the emphasis was on the first syllable, while she said it was on the second.

He called a high-school student who worked in the restaurant over to their table and asked, "Please, very slowly, tell us where we are."

The high-school student stepped back, looked at the couple and said very slowly, "Bur. . .ger. . .King!"

An older minister was advising a younger minister. "You will discover," he said, "that in nearly every group there is at least one person who will want to argue with you."

"What shall I do?" queried the young minister.

"Well," the senior adult replied, "your first impression will be to cut him off or put him down. However, I advise you to think very carefully before doing that. He is probably the only one who is listening."

In a domestic-relations court, the judge listened intently to both sides in a case against an elderly man who was charged by his wife with nonsupport.

After all the evidence was in, the judge told the defendant: "You haven't taken proper care of this good woman and I'm going to give her $100 a month."

The defendant beamed with pleasure. "That's mighty nice of you, Judge," he said, "and I'll give her a few dollars from time to time myself."

Baldness

Question: What is a bald man's greatest wish?

Answer: Dandruff.

He got up every morning and went through the same ritual. He ran his fingers through his thinning hair and complained about losing it. Then he started counting his hairs every morning. The countdown was almost on a daily basis. His wife could hear him saying, "Ten, nine, eight, seven, six, five, four, three, two, one."

Finally, one day he emerged from the bathroom and screamed, "Oh no, I'm bald!"

Senior Adult: "I take great comfort in the fact that they don't put marble tops on cheap tables."

Junior Adult: "Unfortunately, they are found primarily on antiques."

The older a man gets, the more ways he learns to part his hair. Some men pull what little bit of hair they have around on their head to cover their baldness. However, as a man gets even older, he realizes there are basically only three ways to wear your hair —parted, unparted, and departed.

Bulges (Dieting)

If you think old soldiers just fade away, try getting into your old uniform.

"Did you know that being overweight is not hereditary."
"No, I didn't know that."
"Being overweight is not hereditary, but it sure shows up in your jeans!"

You know you are eating too much when you have more jiggle than jog when you run.

When allowing yourself to gain too much weight, and you want to appear as though you really don't care, just say this to your friends, "I'd rather plump up than dry up!"

You know, doctors say if we eat slower we will eat less. Big deal! We all learned that during the Depression as members of a large family.

The Public Health Service reports that there are at least 5 million overweight people in the United States—that's in round figures, of course.

The thirty-day diet is quite popular— that's the one people are going to start in about thirty days.

The pleasures of eating are fleeting.
But the pleasures of fasting are lasting.

There's one thing that will give you more for your money than it did ten years ago— the penny scale at the corner drugstore.

If at first you don't recede, diet, diet again.

The best place for your bathroom scales is in front of your refrigerator.

A sign in a reducing salon read: "PLEASE DO NOT FEED THE CUSTOMERS."

Diets are for persons who are thick and tired of it all.

A diet is what you keep putting off while you keep putting on.

Two kids were examining some bathroom scales. "What's it for?" one asked.

"I don't know," the other answered. "I think you stand on it and it makes you mad."

Dieting is slowing down to make a curve.

"What do you think of Medicare?" someone asked a backwoods woman.
"Oh, I like it a lot," she replied. "I took it for a month and lost ten pounds."

Changes

John Latta has shared with us how teenage slang has changed from 1920 to 1980:

1980's

Nuke—To microwave
Mickey Ds—Hamburgers
Smoke head—One who smokes
Ditz or airhead—A stupid person
Blow-off—To disregard, ignore, or not try
Dude—A person
Nerd, geek—An undesirable person, a loser
History—Gone or leaving ("I'm history")
Bottle it—Get to the point
Veg out, blob out, veg—To do completely nothing

Chill out—Relax, calm down

1950's

I'll be a dirty bird!—I'll be doggoned
Crazy—Wow
Real gone—Really great
Dig—Appreciate
Cool cat—Suave fellow
Bread—Money
Classy chassis—good-looking body
The most—The best
Bobby soxer—Girl
Plastered—Drunk

1920's

Hot mama—Wild woman
The bee's knees, the cat's pajamas—Out of
   this world
Flapper—Free-spirited young woman
It—Sex appeal
Jazz beau—Fashionable man
Hep cat—Someone in style
Illuminated, fried, crocked, lit up like Times
   Square—Drunk

Since I was born some years ago
This world has changed somehow.
We use both milk and butter
That has never seen a cow.
We have instant coffee, instant tea,
Instant this and instant that;

Lots of other instant foods
Not fit to feed a cat.
We have substitute sugar, substitute salt;
We have so many substitutes
We don't know who to fault.
Boys and girls both dress alike;
Can't tell one from the other.
Same way with Mom and Dad,
Can't tell Dad from Mother.
One more thing that don't look right;
I think that it's a sin.
They've moved the cook stove out of doors
And moved the outhouse in!
I don't know how far this will go,
But up until this minute,
I love this good old world of ours
'Cause I can still live in it.

—Author Unknown

G. Othel Hand wrote a beautiful satire on the use of words, entitled, "What's Happening to the King's English?"

Remember when "hippie" meant big in the hips,
And a "trip" involved cars, planes, and ships.
And "pot" was a vessel for cooking things in,
And "hooked" was what Grandmother's rug might have been.

When "neat" meant well organized, tidy
and clean
And "grass" was a ground cover, normally
green.
When "lights," and not people, were
turned on and off.
And the "pill" could be what you took for
a cough.
When "fuzz" was a substance fluffy like
lint,
And "bread" came from bakeries, not from
the mint.
When "square" meant a ninety-degree
angle form,
And "cool" was a temperature not quite
warm.
When "roll" was a bun, and "rock" was a
stone,
And "hang-up" was what you could do
with the phone.
When "chicken" meant poultry and "bag"
meant a sack,
And "junk," trashy cast-offs and old bric-
a-brac.
When "swinger" was someone who
swung in a swing.
And "pad" was a soft, sort of cushiony
thing.
When "dig" meant to shovel and spade in
the dirt,
And "put-on" was what you would do
with a shirt.
Words once so sensible, sober, and serious,

Are making the freak scene like psycho
    delirious.
It's groovy, man, groovy, but English it's
    not;
Me thinks that the language has gone
    straight to pot!

Church (Ministers)

A pastor finished a glowing message one
Sunday morning. A stately grandmother
with her young grandson shook the pastor's
hand at the back door and announced, "Oh,
Pastor, I'm just filled with your message!"

The pastor, quite embarrassed with such
a response, turned to the little boy and
asked, "Well, Young Man, what did you
think of the sermon?"

The little boy looked up at the pastor and
said, "To be honest, Pastor, I got a belly full
of you, too!"

The only time the pastor ever sees some
people is when they're hatched, matched,
or dispatched!

I took my small grandson to church. He
watched as the choir came out of the side

door in white robes and took their places. Then he leaned over to me and whispered, "Look, Granddaddy! They're all going to get a haircut."

We church members are often like the farmer's well that freezes up in the winter and dries up in the summer.

I met a neighbor on the street and said, "Hey, Bill! I didn't see you in church, Sunday."

"Of course, you didn't," he replied, "I was taking up the collection."

Old Granny was eighty-seven and her health was very poor, but she definitely would not consent to see a doctor. Finally, her granddaughter requested her family physician to come to the house and examine her grandmother thoroughly.

After the doctor had taken his leave, Granny yelled for her granddaughter.

"Betty," she said, "who in the world was that nice young preacher?"

"Well, I have to confess, Granny," said the granddaughter, "that was no preacher— he was a doctor."

"A doctor!" exclaimed the grandmother with great disappointment. "Well, I thought he looked a little too familiar to be a preacher!"

One preacher said that when the resurrection takes place he knew his church members would beat all others out of the grave, because the Bible says, "the dead in Christ shall rise first."

Church typewriters are notorious for embarrassing blunders in church bulletins. One that should have used the word "life," printed the sermon topic: "How to Change Your Wife Through Prayer." When the error was shown to the pastor, he said, "Let it alone. Someone might need it."

Another church bulletin, intending to use "take," had the pastor's column read: "Many calls come to the church each week and we conscientiously fake an interest in every one of them."

A Sunday School teacher described to her class how Lot's wife looked back and turned into a pillar of salt.

"Aw, that's nothing," one little boy interrupted. "My mommy looked back and turned into a telephone pole!"

I was pastoring in a small town of about twelve-hundred folks after graduating from Seminary. I had a lot of stored-up knowledge to dispose of. On the Sunday before the Fourth of July, I preached a rip-roaring sermon with strong patriotic over-tones.

Several people joined the church that morning. My six-year-old son went down the line of new members, shaking their hands vigorously and saying, "God bless you in the name of the United States of America!"

A church advertised: "Earth's last war! Where will it be fought? At the Adventist Church Sunday Night!"

Once my sweet little wife suggested that when I prepare my sermon to remember the advertisement of a new washing machine: "After it spins dry, it shuts itself off au-tomatically."

The Sunday School teacher explained to the little boys in the class that "Lot was warned to take his wife and flee from the city, but his wife turned to salt."

"What happened to the flea?" one little boy asked.

Once while I was preaching a man in the back row shouted, "I can't hear you!"

Another man seated down front got up and shouted back, "I can! Come up here and I'll gladly change places with you!"

Confusion

Psychologist—A man who tells you something you already know in words that you can't understand.

The following are actual excuses submitted by parents in one northeastern Pennsylvania school district:

"Dear School: Please ackuse [sic] John for being absent January 28, 29, 30, 31, 32, 33."

"I kept Billy Home because she had to go Christmas shopping because I didn't know what size she wear."

"My son is under the doctor's care and should not take P.E. Please execute [sic] him."

"Please excuse Joyce from P.E. for a few days. Yesterday she fell out of a tree and misplaced her hip."

"Please excuse Jimmy from being. It was his father's fault."

A doctor, writing in the usual scribbled fashion, gave a prescription to one of his patients. The patient put it in his pocket and forgot to have it filled.

Two years later, he pulled it out of his pocket, showed it to a bus driver, and received a free ride to a neighboring city. He decided to press his luck and was allowed to enter an art museum, several movies, and a Broadway musical.

He flashed it a time or two at restaurants and received a 20 percent discount on his meals. One day his granddaughter happened to pick it up and play it on the piano, and she won a scholarship to the conservatory of music.

From the California Newspaper Publishers Association, here is an example of a typographical error in the classified section of a small-town newspaper, and the subsequent disastrous attempts to correct it:

(Monday)) "**FOR SALE**—R. D. Jones has one sewing machine for sale. Phone 948-0707 after 7 PM and ask for Mrs. Kelly who lives with him cheap."

(Tuesday) "**NOTICE**—We regret having erred in R. D. Jones's ad yesterday. It should have read: 'One sewing machine for sale. Cheap. Phone 948-0707 and ask for Mrs. Kelly who lives with him after 7 PM.' "

(Wednesday) "**NOTICE**—R. D. Jones has

informed us that he has received several annoying telephone calls because of the error we made in his classified ad yesterday. His ad stands correct as follows: 'FOR SALE— R. D. Jones has one sewing machine for sale. Cheap. Phone 948-0707 PM and ask for Mrs. Kelly who loves with him.' "

(Thursday)"**NOTICE**—I, R. D. Jones, have *no* sewing machine for sale. I *smashed it.* Don't call 948-0707, as the telephone has been out. I have *not* been carrying on with Mrs. Kelly. Until yesterday she was my housekeeper, but she quit.' "

"Raymond," said the doctor, "you look worse! The last time you came to see me I instructed you to drink warm water an hour before each meal. Now, have you been doing it?"

"Honestly, Doctor, I have tried and tried to do what you told me," replied the patient, "but I can only keep it up for about twenty minutes!"

A cowboy said to a city slicker, "Hey, fellow, you're getting your saddle on backwards, aren't you?"

"That's what you think," the city dude replied. "You don't know which way I'm going."

A young woman, tired of hearing her parents telling her to get married, joined the Peace Corps and was sent to Africa. She cabled her parents she was getting married.

A large reception was planned to welcome the newlyweds. The big day finally came. Their daughter stepped off the plane and directly behind her walked a Zulu witch doctor, dressed in feathers and paint.

"No, dear!" cried the horrified mother, "I said a rich doctor, not a witch doctor!"

One day two men, clad in hospital gowns, sat in the office of an emergency room. "I only wanted to have my eyes examined," complained one.

"You're lucky," replied the other. "I just came in to read the meter!"

One day he looked up from his racing form and noticed the baby in the playpen. Turning to his wife he yelled, "Baby's nose is running again!"

"My goodness!" she snapped, "Don't you ever think of anything but race horses?"

Have you ever wondered why Noah didn't swat both flies when he had a chance?

The doctor grabbed his coat and hat and started out the front door. "I've got to go," he explained to his teenage daughter. "Some man on the phone just said he couldn't live without me!"

"Just a minute, Dad!" she replied. "I believe that call was for me."

Courting

They had just celebrated their fiftieth anniversary. As they were driving across town to their home, she remarked, "You know, we used to sit closer to each other in the car in our courting days over fifty years ago."

"I haven't moved!" he exclaimed.

On their sixtieth wedding anniversary, a reporter came to interview them. "What big problems have you had in your marriage?" he asked the elderly woman.

"Well, there's really been only two—Pa and the fire."

"What do you mean, 'Pa and the fire'?" asked the reporter.

With a gleam in her eye, she explained, "When I paid too much attention to one the other went out!"

My grandson wanted to know if I could remember my first kiss.

"Son," I replied, "I can't even remember my last one!"

I say, keep the glow in your relationship. Don't be like the postman who always talked shop at home. It was "Post Office this, and Post Office that."

Finally, his wife had had enough and said, "You spend all day working at the Post Office, then you spend all night talking about the Post Office. The trouble with you is you've forgotten how to play 'Post Office'!"

An elderly woman was telling her daughter about a date with a ninety-year-old man. "Would you believe, I had to slap his face three times."

"Do you mean," the daughter asked in disgust, "that old man got fresh with you?"

"Oh, no!" her mother explained, "I had to keep slapping his face to keep him awake."

A man was walking along a road, and a woman was walking on another. The roads came together at a juncture and the man and woman walked along side by side.

He was carrying a large, iron kettle on his

back. In one hand he held a chicken by the legs, in the other a cane, and he was leading a goat.

As they neared a dark ravine the woman stopped and said, "I'm afraid to go through that dark ravine with you. You might overpower me and kiss me by force."

"How can I possibly overpower you and kiss you," the man pointed out, "with an iron kettle on my back, a cane and a chicken in my hands, and leading a goat?"

"Easy," she replied. "If you stick the cane in the ground and tie your goat to it, then turn the kettle upside down and put the chicken under it, then you might kiss me in spite of my resistance."

Sure enough when they entered the dark ravine, he stuck the cane in the ground, tied the goat to it, and handed the chicken to the woman saying, "Hold it while I cut some grass for the goat."

And—as the story goes—he lowered the kettle from his shoulders, put the chicken under it, and kissed the woman as she knew he would.

> Oh, the innocent victims of Cupid,
> Remember this terse little verse:
> "To let a fool kiss you is stupid,
> To let a kiss fool you is worse."

Just remember, kissing is a do-it-yourself job. Don't be like the man who hadn't kissed his wife in twenty years—but shot the man who did!

In her later years the famous actress Sarah Bernhardt lived in an apartment high over Paris. An old admirer climbed all the stairs to see her one day. He asked her breathlessly, "Why do you live so high up?"

"Dear friend," she replied, "it is the only way I can still make the hearts of men beat faster."

> Everything was going fine;
> Quite romantic and dandy.
> Until this year when
> He sent me dietetic candy.

Marriage is an investment that pays you dividends if you pay interest.

Death

Man: "Can I come over later today to make arrangements for my wife's funeral service?"

Funeral director: "Your wife? Didn't we bury her three years ago?"

Man: "Yeah, we did. However, I married again."

Funeral director: "Well, congratulations!"

It's not good for your health to think of yourself too much. You might die laughing.

Zeb: "I didn't know that your son was a funeral director. I thought you said he was a doctor."

Zeke: "Well, no, I only told you that he followed the medical profession!"

Family Doctor—One who prevents you from dying a natural death.

Pathologist—One who tells your family what you were being cured of when you died.

Consultant—Another doctor who is called in at the last minute to share the blame.

Everyone knew he was a worthless culprit. At his funeral, however, that pastor went on and on eulogizing the man.

After listening for a while, his wife leaned over to one of his sons and said, "Go over there and see if that's your dad in that casket."

"Now, Rachel," the doctor informed his patient, "there is absolutely no doubt that you will fully recover."

"But why are you so sure?" replied Rachel. "You said before that this was an extremely serious disease with the odds against me!"

"Quite right," replied the doctor. "My medical guidebook clearly states that eleven out of every twelve patients with your illness succumb to it."

"This doesn't reassure me, Doctor," replied Rachel shakily.

"Oh, well, it should," answered the physician. "You see, you are the twelfth patient I've treated with this disease—and the first eleven died!"

An old grumpy doctor with a none too good reputation died, oddly enough, in poverty.

His few friends decided to solicit donations for the burial and proceeded to ask several of his patients. Unfortunately, the very first they asked was an old man equally as disagreeable as the doctor and who had no liking for the medical profession.

"What have you scavengers put me down for?" scowled the old man.

"Ten dollars is what we would like," quickly replied one of them.

The old man took out his checkbook, wrote a check for $120.00 and added sarcastically, "Now, go get busy and bury a dozen of them!"

Two older widow ladies were talking in the lounge of their retirement village. "Well," one said, "Jane has just cremated her third husband."

"Yeah, that's the way it goes," replied the other widow, "Some of us can't find a husband, and others have husbands to burn!"

A bloated old physician was delivering a rather boring speech to a club group. The speech described physicians as a group of slaves to mankind who worked long and hard to relieve suffering. He continued, "but we are at the mercy of society and unfortunately have many critics in this world."

"Not to mention," replied a voice in the crowd, "many more in the next!"

Comedian Woody Allen once said, "I'm not afraid of dying. I just don't want to be there when it happens."

Dr. Williams was on his deathbed and Rev. Crout asked him to confess his sins before he went to his reward.

The old doctor stammered, "Well, I never could resist gambling. . . lost a lot of money, in fact; and I guess I have overcharged most of my patients. . . operated on some that didn't need the operation; and I just never could overcome my desire to have an affair with the good-looking women, and I lied to my wife all our life. . . I never had thought about it before, but I guess I was a pretty lousy person!"

The minister folded his hands and smiled knowingly and said, "Now, my Son, I think you should renounce the devil."

"Now wait just a minute, Preacher," the old man wheezed. "This ain't no time for me to antagonize anybody!"

A young upstart insurance salesman was trying to sell a ninety-five-year-old man an insurance policy. "No, I'm not interested," said the kindly old gentleman. "I don't plan to live that long."

"Well," said the insurance salesman, "we have a special today on a ten-year insurance policy."

"No," the old man said, "I don't plan to live that long."

"Well, Sir, it is my privilege to inform

you that my company has just issued a brand new five-year policy and you'll be the first one to receive this offer."

The ninety-five-year-old man smiled and said calmly, "Look, Young Man, you don't seem to understand. At my age, I don't even buy green bananas!"

Seventy-five-year-old man: "When I die I hope it is in a hurry. I'd be satisfied to die in the crash of a speeding car."

Eighty-five-year-old man: "I think it would be better to die in a plane crash."

Ninety-five-year-old man: "I've got a better idea than either of you—I'd rather die from smoke inhalation from blowing out 100 candles on my birthday cake."

"Grandma, what happens when we die?"

"Well," his grandma explained, "God forms us from the dust and we are born. When we die, our bodies turn back to dust."

Later that day her grandson found a pile of dirt under the bed. He ran screaming, "Grandma! Come quick! Somebody's under the bed either coming or going."

"You're not telling me something, are you, Doctor?" she inquired. "I just know you think I'm going to die!"

"Now, Madam," replied the doctor, "you have merely had the flu and you're almost well."

"Are you sure?" questioned the woman. "Why, I've heard of people dying because the doctor didn't diagnose their disease correctly!"

"When I diagnose the flu, that's what they die of!" exclaimed the doctor.

A gentleman was getting a little nervous after a three-doctor bedside conference. The nurse had to ask one of the doctors to return.

"Do calm yourself down," soothed the doctor. "Why have you gotten so excited?"

"Well, it was all that arguing by you three doctors as to what was wrong with me. You all must not know what is wrong with me, and I'm worried," answered the patient.

"Oh, don't pay any attention to those other doctors," replied the physician. "They don't know—but I do, and I am positive the autopsy will prove me correct!"

"Old Mr. Grumpy looks like he won't be with us much longer, Nurse," said the doctor. "One might say he already has one foot in the grate."

46

"Don't you mean one foot in the *grave?*" asked the nurse.

"Well no," answered the doctor. "You see he plans to be cremated!"

"Frank, I know I am dying," a woman said to her husband. "Now, I want you to grant me a last request. Will you ride to my funeral in the same car with my mother?"

"Ok, I'll do it," replied the husband, "but I know it's gonna ruin my whole day!"

I grew up in a little town in the South. The name of our funeral home was "Southern Planters."

If husbands want to die with their boots on, they should try wearing them on the newly-cleaned carpet.

"When I am dead you'll find it hard," said
   he,
"To ever find another man like me."
"What makes you think," said she, "as I
   suppose you do,
I'd ever want another man like you!"

One day I became quite ill. My wife called the doctor. He examined me and said, "I can get you well. You'll need test, X-rays, and an operation. It'll cost about five thousand dollars."

"Don't bother, Doc," I replied. "I got a better offer yesterday from the undertaker."

Definitions

Parking Space—An area which disappears as you are making a U-turn.

Highbrow—A person educated beyond their intelligence.

Social Grace—When you start out on the right foot rather than putting it in your mouth.

Charity—That generous impulse to give away something you have no use for.

Conceit—A form of "I" strain.

Flattery—The art of telling a person exactly what he thinks of himself.

Memory—The thing I forget with.

Skiing—Something you learn in many sittings.

Alimony—The fee a woman charges for name dropping.

Relatives—People who come to dinner who aren't friends.

Proverb—A short sentence based on long experience.

Laziness—The habit of resting before you get tired.

Prejudice—Weighing the facts with your thumb on the scale.

Social Tact—Making people feel at home when you wish they were.

Poise—The ability to keep talking while the other person picks up the check.

Parking Meter—A piggy bank on a hitching post.

Small Town—A place where it's no sooner done than said.

Committee—A group that keeps minutes and wastes hours.

Childhood—That happy period when nightmares occur only during sleep.

Small Town—A place where the postmaster knows more than the schoolmaster, but not as much as the telephone operator.

Egotism—The art of seeing qualities in yourself which others can't see.

Egotist—A conceited person who thinks he knows as much as you do.

Egotism—That which enables a man who is in a rut to think he's "in the groove."

Diplomacy—Saying, "nice doggy," while you're looking around for a rock.

Girdle—An ingenious device invented to keep an unfortunate situation from spreading.

Egotist—A person who thinks if he hadn't been born, people would wonder why.

Diet—Something to take the starch out of you.

Prune—A plum that has seen better days.

Waitress—A person who thinks money grows on trays.

Old Age—A time of life when men pay more attention to the food than they do to the waitress.

Parents—People who *bear* infants, *bore* teenagers, and *board* newlyweds.

Doctors (Illness)

The Three stages of getting sick: ill, pill, bill.

Practicing Physician—Unfortunately for the patient, any doctor until he retires.

"That pain in your leg is caused by old age," the doctor told his elderly patient.

"That can't be," said the man. "The other leg is the same age and it doesn't hurt a bit."

Doctor's Receptionist—One who methodically arranges patient's appointments so that the maximum amount of contagious diseases may be transferred in the waiting room to the maximum number of patients in a minimum amount of time.

"Oh, I had a pitiful case today," Dr. Hack informed his wife. "One of the patients died after he drank a quart of varnish."

"What a horrible end," replied his wife.

"A horrible end, yes," said the doctor, "but a glossy finish!"

I know a doctor who will not operate unless it is absolutely necessary—unless he absolutely needs the money.

"Now, John," said the psychiatrist, "you've been seeing me for months and you seem to be getting worse. What is your problem?"

"It's this terrible feeling of not belonging," cried the patient. "Since paying all your bills, my house doesn't belong to me, my car doesn't belong to me, my. . .!"

During the peak of the cold and virus season last winter, my doctor was giving a lot of penicillin shots. Tacked to the door of his office was a sign that read; "To Save Time, Please Back into the Office."

After quite a bout, my doctor said, "You've been a very sick man. In fact, it was your strong constitution that pulled you through."

"That's good to know," I replied. "I trust you will keep that in mind when you make out my bill."

Do you know what a specialist is? He's a doctor who has his patients trained to become ill only during office hours.

Driving

It takes hundreds of nuts to hold a car together but only one to scatter it all over the highway.

Somebody asked me how long it took for my wife to learn to drive. "Come this fall," I replied, "it will be three years."

I remember teaching her to drive. "Go on green," I explained. "Stop on red, and take it easy when my face turns white."

Just kidding. My wife is just as good a driver as I am—and she can do it on either side of the road.

She's really careful, and always looks both ways before going through a red light. I wouldn't say she has had a lot of accidents, but I call her car "The Bullet"—it's all shot!

But she's prepared for an emergency. That's why she always drives with the emergency brake on.

Once on a trip while she was driving the brakes failed going down a steep grade. "I can't stop!" She screamed. "What shall I do?"

"Brace yourself, Darling," I shouted, "and hit something cheap."

Once the taillight of her car went out, but she got it fixed. She stopped at the service station and had the man add a quart of red oil.

One day a policeman stopped her and said, "Lady, you were traveling sixty miles an hour."

"It's not possible," she insisted, "I've only been driving twenty minutes."

The other day she put a penny in a parking meter and bent down to take a look. "Oh, my goodness!" she exclaimed, "I've lost 100 pounds!"

One day I was driving. My wife was sitting beside me and my mother-in-law was in the back seat. Both were giving me instructions. Finally, I had had enough. I stopped the car and said to my wife, "Now, I want to know who is driving this car? You or your mother?"

But I say, the wife who drives from the backseat of a car is no worse than the husband who cooks from the dining room table. Amen!

Most accidents are caused by motorists who drive in high while their minds are in neutral.

I took my aunt out riding,
Though icy was the breeze;
I put her in the rumble seat,
To see my auntie freeze.

My driving is perfection,
My courtesy is tops;
I just caught the reflection
Of a motorcycle cop.

Have you ever noticed that the only time a car's windshield wiper works perfectly is when it's holding a parking ticket?

Eating (Food, Cooking)

Food prices are going up so fast that it's soon going to be cheaper to eat the money.

Isn't it too bad we don't retain as much of what we read as what we eat?

My wife makes good enthusiastic stew—she puts everything she has into it.
And you ought to taste her Lucifer cake. It was supposed to be angel food cake, but it fell.
She's thoughtful, too. She sets my plate

before me and says, "There you are, darling. It's cooked just the way you'd better like it!"

She baked two kinds of biscuits last night. When she passed them to me, she asked, "Would you like to take your pick?"

"No, thanks, honey," I replied. "I'll just use my hammer."

I'm not saying her cooking is bad, but penciled on the wall of our kitchen are the words: "Duncan Hines wept here!"

Every evening when I get home I greet my wife with a kiss and say, "Hi, Honey, what's thawing?"

She has cookbooks by the dozen. They're such fascinating reading. They have so many stirring things in them.

I complained to my wife, "Where does all that grocery money go?"

"Stand sideways and look in the mirror," she replied.

I'll give her credit. She knows how to serve company. She can fix food either way —so they'll come back or so they won't.

There's a new Chinese restaurant for dieters. They serve all the food you can eat for fifty cents. Trouble is—they only give you one chopstick.

Adam and Eve had the only perfect marriage. That was because he didn't have to hear about all the men she could have married; and she didn't have to hear about the way his mother cooked!"

My wife and I were trying to eat in one of those rock-and-roll joints. I'm not saying the music was bad, but when a waiter dropped a tray of dishes, six couples got up to dance.

What keeps most would-be investors out of the stock market is the supermarket.

Epitaphs

Epitaph on a hypochondriac's grave—"I Told You I Was Sick."

A California lawyer's gravestone read: "Final Decree."

A henpecked Illinois lawyer listed the names of his three wives, then proclaimed: "The Defense Rests."

A newsman's epitaph said, "Copy All In."

An Iowa traveling salesman ordered:

"My Trip Is Ended. Send My Samples Home."

The family of a railroad man carved this question on his stone: "Papa, Did You Wind Your Watch?"

An Indiana teacher had a brief memorial: "School Is Out. Teacher Has Gone Home."

An avid baseball fan said it in two words: "Play Ball!"

An unhappy wife bequeathed a few choice lines: "After Having Lived With Her Husband for Some 65 Years, She Died in Hopes of a Better Life."

Exercise (Fitness)

He was in good shape even though he was ninety years of age. Knowing that he was a former body-builder and great athlete, a newspaper reporter asked, "What exercise do you do to stay fit?"

"My boy," replied the old man, "when you're pushing ninety, that's the only exercise you need!"

A reporter was interviewing a man on his

ninety-ninth birthday. "I certainly hope I can come back next year and see you reach the century mark," he said.

"Can't see any reason why not, Young Feller," the old-timer replied. "You look healthy enough to me!"

They had lived together in the same house for over fifty years. It had been their custom to take an evening walk every day in a open field behind their house.

One evening, they came to a little creek that ran across the open field. "Do you remember how I used to jump that creek flat-footed?"

"Yes," she said, "but that was when we were younger."

"I can still do it," he exclaimed.

Before she could stop him, he took his stance on one side of the creek, squatted down, and leaped forward. Both feet landed squarely in the middle of the creek.

As he waded out of the muddy creek and started back to the house, he commented to his wife, "That's strange! I guess I just didn't notice that creek getting wider through the years."

"You're looking well," said a friend to a ninety-five-year-old former athlete who had kept himself in good shape through the years.

"It's not my appearance that bothers me these days," said the old man, "it's my disappearance!"

Eyesight

His eyesight became worse and worse. Finally, he decided to get a seeing-eye dog. On his first visit to a large department store, he grabbed his dog by the tail and swung it around and around over his head.

A startled clerk ran up to the man and asked, "Sir, what in the world are you doing?"

"Oh, I'm just looking around."

My wife is a strange creature. She can spot a single strand of blond hair on my lapel at fifty feet, and miss a garage door twenty feet wide.

I'm not saying she's jealous, but the other night she couldn't find a single hair on my clothes.

"So!" she screamed. "Now you're running around with a bald-headed woman!"

One of my long-lost uncles who lived in the backwoods finally came out one day and made a trip into town. He attended an auction and saw his first mirror. Looking into it, he thought it was a picture of his dear old pappy.

Naturally, he bought it and slipped it up in the attic where he could sneak a peek now and then.

His suspicious wife noticed his frequent trips to the attic, and while he was out in the field, she slipped up into the attic to investigate. Discovering the mirror, she looked into it and screamed, "So, you're the old hag he's been running around with!"

False Teeth

Many young people don't seem to realize that great truths are spoken through false teeth.

A little girl was fascinated by her grandfather taking out his false teeth and brushing them, so she asked him to do it again. She stood there amazed, then demanded, "Now take off your nose!"

Reflecting on their marriage of over fifty years, he was sitting in his recliner and she was sitting in hers.

"You know," she said, "things have really changed since our marriage."

"How's that?" he asked.

"Well," she said, "you used to sit very close to me instead of in a separate chair.

"Well, I can remedy that," he said as he got up and moved over to one end of the couch."

As she sat on the other end of the couch, she complained, "You used to sit closer to me than this."

"Well," he said, I can remedy that, too," as he moved over close to her.

"You used to put your arm around my shoulders."

"How's that?" he asked, as he put his arm up on the back of the couch.

"Do you remember you used to lean over and nudge my neck with your nose?"

As he nudged her neck with his nose, she had one more complaint, "Darling, don't you remember you used to nibble on my earlobes?"

Quickly, he jumped up and left the room. *Oh my*, she thought to herself. *I've hurt his feelings.*

"Where are you going?" she cried.

"To get my teeth!"

Don't ask me if my cold teeth chatter.
We don't sleep together so it doesn't matter.

The theatre usher quickly dispatched himself down front where a man was crawling around on his hands and knees. "Sir," he said, "you're disturbing several people around you. What's the problem?"

"I've lost my gum!" said the man as he continued to prowl around the seats.

"Sir," the usher said, "if that's your only problem, let me offer you another stick of gum so you can sit down and watch the movie. One stick of gum is not worth all this disturbance."

"But I'm afraid you don't understand," explained the man, "my false teeth are in that gum!"

As the waitress served the elderly couple, she noticed something very unusual. The man began to eat his meal while his wife patiently stared out the window. "Is there anything wrong with your food?" the waitress asked the lady.

"No, the food looks great," she replied.

"Aren't you afraid your food will get cold if you wait much longer to eat?" the waitress queried further.

"Oh," she replied, "that's alright."

"Well, aren't you hungry, Lady," the waitress finally asked.

"I sure am," the lady replied. "I'm just sitting here waiting until my husband gets through with the teeth."

Farming

My cousin lived on a small farm. They called it "Oleo Acres"—it was one of the cheaper spreads.

They raised hogs instead of corn and potatoes. "Because," my cousin explained, "hogs don't take no hoein'."

Once I visited my country cousin and helped with the milking. I must have done good. I got milk out of three spigots.

I guess I was ignorant of country life. I pointed and asked my cousin why that cow didn't have horns. "Well, there are several reasons," he explained. "Some cows don't have horns until later in life. Others have them removed. And still others are born without them. But this one doesn't have any horns because it's a horse."

One afternoon I climbed a fence into a pasture and saw a vicious-looking bull.

"Hey!" I called to my cousin. "Is this bull safe?"

"Yep!" replied my cousin. "He's a heap safer than you are!"

I feel sad for farmers. Potato bugs ruin potato crops, and corn borers destroy corn. Pity those poor dairy farmers with butterflies everywhere.

My cousin's wife called the druggist and ordered some powerful medicine for her husband and her horse.

"Be sure and write plain on them labels which is for the horse and which is for my husband," she instructed. "I don't want nothin' to happen to that horse before spring plowin'."

Once my country cousin came to visit me in the city. He was fascinated by the paved streets. Digging his heel into the hard surface he said, "Can't blame you folks for building a town here. This ground sure ain't fittin' to plow!"

Finances (Inflation, Banking, Budgets)

Some say that no person should keep too much to oneself. The IRS is of the same opinion.

A balanced budget is when the earning power catches up with the yearning capacity.

This is the land of plenty—everything here costs plenty.

Dr. Sawbones confronted Mrs. Hypochondriac about the bills she hadn't been paying.

"I'm very sorry about this," the doctor tried to explain, "but I don't see how I can continue to treat you because your bill is much more than it should be."

"Well, I'm certainly glad you have come to your senses, doctor," she cried. "Now, if you'll just make your bill out for what it should be, I'll write you a check!"

Stock Market Advice: It's not the bulls and bears you have to watch out for—it's the bum steers.

In modern finance things are touch and go. First, they touch you for the money, then you wonder where it goes.

It's not the rat race that's a bother; it's the high price of the cheese.

Money may not buy happiness, but long-term leases are available.

Obstetrician—A doctor who doesn't believe that all people should be born free.

Practical Nurse—One who marries a wealthy patient.

"My doctor vowed that he would have me walking in three months," said George.
"And did he succeed?" inquired a friend.
"You bet he did!" answered George. "With what he charged me, I had to sell my car!"

We have an all-electric home—everything is charged.

Money still talks but you have to increase the volume if you want to get the message through.

When my son was in college he sent me this letter:

"Dear Dad,

Gue$$ what I need mo$t of all? That'$ right. $end it along.
Be$t wi$he$,
Your $on,
Ru$$."

I replied:

"Dear Russ,

I'm glad to kNOw that you are NOt doing badly in college. NOthing pleases me more. Write aNOther letter soon. As I have NO news, I must close NOw.
Dad."

One of my girlfriends jilted me when I told her about my rich uncle. Now she's my aunt.

It takes a long time to pay out a new car. The other day I saw an ad that read: "For Sale '29 Model A Ford. Take over payments."

The thing to buy for a man who has everything is a calendar to remind him when the payments are due.

A door-to-door salesman said to my wife, "Let me show you something your neighbor said you couldn't afford."

Financing a household today is like a three-ring circus. While I'm trying to balance the accounts, my wife juggles the budget, and the banker bounces my checks.

The old woman who lived in a shoe now has a lot of descendants who are living on a shoestring.

Parents of a large number of children deserve a lot of credit; in fact, they can't get along without it.

Remember that sales talk is trade wind.

The futility of riches is plainly stated in the Bible and the income-tax form.

Income Tax is Uncle Sam's version of "Truth or Consequences."
The tax office in the little town had a sign over the door as you entered that read, "Watch Your Step."
As you left, the back of the same sign read, "Watch Your Language."

My successful uncle lay dying. He gave instructions to have his body cremated after death, and the ashes placed in an envelope and sent to the IRS with a note, "Now you have everything."

The difference between the short and

long income tax forms is simple. If you use the short form, the government gets your money. If you use the long form, the accountant gets your money.

Gardening

Question: What do you learn when buying a load of topsoil?
Answer: That while some things are dirt cheap, dirt is not one of them.

A man stopped by to see an old couple he hadn't visited in a long time. "How's John?" he asked the woman.

"Oh," she explained, "didn't you know he's dead? He went down to the garden to pull a cabbage for dinner. When he bent down, he fell dead, right there on the spot."

"That's terrible," the visitor replied. "What on earth did you do?"

"Well, what *could* we do?" the old woman answered. "We had to open a can of peas!"

My uncle Al doesn't know much about plants. Once a neighbor was showing him through her new green house.

"This plant belongs to the Begonia family," she explained.

"Oh," gushed my uncle, "how nice of you to look after it while they're away!"

I'm not much of a gardener. Once I took a seed catalog and started out the door.

"Where are you going with that?" my wife asked.

"I'm going to show it to my tomatoes," I explained.

To cultivate a garden takes too much time and labor;
I'd rather live next door to one and cultivate my neighbor.

My grandfather was a farmer. He didn't claim to know much, but he always had a good crop. Once a student from the state agricultural college came out.

"Your methods of cultivation are hopelessly out of date," the young man said. "Why I'd be surprised if you get ten pounds of apples off that tree."

"So would I," my grandfather responded. "It's a pear tree!"

Farming helps a farmer remember dates. Once a census taker asked a farmer the birthdate of his daughter.

"Well," he drawled, "she was born 'bout 'tater time, but I'll be hanged if I can remember if it was diggin' or plantin' time!"

My aunt, whose elevator doesn't go all the way to the top, wrote the Agriculture Department a letter:

"Dear Sirs:

"Could you send me a booklet explaining the use of different poisons for vegetables in the garden? I have lost my husband, and I have lots of different poisons on hand."

Gossip

There's a good thing about putting your foot in your mouth. You won't step on anyone's toes.

Have you ever noticed that every time a man tells a doctor that he is all tired out, the first thing he examines is his tongue!

Gossip is the art of making a mountain out of a molehill by piling on the dirt. It's letting the "chat" out of the bag. It's a newscaster without a sponsor. And the difference between gossip and news depends on whether you heard it or told it.

A little girl in Sunday School proudly quoted the memory verse: "Go ye into all the world and preach the gossip."

A neighbor in our area said to her friend next door, "You know, I wouldn't say anything about Rosy unless it was good—and, oh boy, is this good!"

Her motto is: "If you can't say anything good about a person, let's hear it."

Gossip results when we throw our jaw in gear before our brain is turning over. We forget that our tongue is in a wet place and likely to slip.

Have you noticed that a person usually leads with his chin when his mouth is wide open? And isn't it strange how often small talk comes in large doses.

When some folks hold a conversation, they forget to turn it loose. Some will never learn that the best way to save face is to stop shooting it off. Their idea of keeping a secret is refusing to tell who told it to them.

Two things are really bad for the heart—running up stairs and down people.

When dial telephones were installed out where my country cousin lives, telephone personnel came out to teach the rural people how to use the new equipment.

After lengthy instructions, my cousin's wife asked the telephone representative, "I just have one question: What number do I dial when I want to listen in?"

Some folks don't have much to say, but you have to listen a long time to find it out. Blessed are they who have nothing to say—and cannot be persuaded to say it.

> I'm careful of the words I say,
> I keep them soft and sweet.
> I never know from day to day
> Which ones I'll have to eat.

Out of the mouths of babes will come words they should never have heard us say in the first place.

Many friends are like a team of horses—parted by a tongue.

We have to be real careful with half-truths; we will likely repeat the wrong half.

A gossip is a person with a sense of rumor. And that's as hard to unspread as butter.

Grandchildren, Grandparents

Satisfied Grandmother—If she had it to do all over again, she would bypass children and just have grandchildren.

Her grandchild was a teenager before she actually met him. They hugged and kissed and the teenager said, "So you're my grandmother?"

"Yes," she replied, "I'm your grandmother on your father's side."

The teenager replied, "Well, I can tell you right now—you're on the wrong side!"

The proud grandfather was driving his granddaughter through the countryside pointing out agricultural points of interest.

He pointed to a herd of cattle. "Aren't those beautiful?" be asked.

"Yes, Paw-paw," said his granddaughter. "What kind of cows are those?"

"Jersey cows," explained the grandfather.

"How can you tell?" the granddaughter

75

asked. "They're not wearing any license plates!"

Question: Why did God never plan for grandparents to have babies?
Answer: Because they might lay a baby down and forget where they put it.

Grandfather: "Is there anything worse than being old and bent?"
College Grandson: "Yes, being young and broke!"

Grandfather on airplane: "Have I told you about my grandchildren?"
Occupant in the next seat: "No, and I certainly do appreciate it!"

An old doctor was turning his practice over to his grandson, fresh out of medical school. After a couple of weeks of vacation, the old doctor returned to hear what the younger doctor thought was good news.

"Guess what, Grandad," he exclaimed. "Do you remember Mrs. Williams who has been coming to you for indigestion for thirty years? While you were gone, I prescribed some medicine and she has been cured."

The older doctor moaned, "Son, that indigestion put you through college and medical school!"

There's nothing more affectionate than grandchildren with sticky hands. And they leave a trail wherever they go. As someone put it:

Our rugs and floors give evidence,
Enough to wear our patience thin,
That one small boy with two small feet
Can bring so much of the outdoors in!

Sometimes kids misbehave. I say, if brushing up on manners doesn't help a child, the brush ought to be moved down.

Seeing the way kids act these days, it's obvious many parents embarked on the sea of matrimony without a paddle.

Everybody in the neighborhood was talking about the new painless dentist in town. I sent my grandson, who is something of a problem in a dentist's chair.

When he got back he said proudly, "Aw, he's not painless at all. He put his finger in my mouth, and I bit it, and he yelled like all the others!"

A baby has a way of making a man out

of his father and a boy out of his grand-father.

Grandchildren are God's reward for growing older.

In spite of all their messin'
Grandchildren are a blessin'

Health (Hospitals, Pain)

If hospitals are places to get well, why do they serve that food?

Minor Operation—Any operation that someone else has.

Nurse: "Doctor, how was the operation?"
Doctor: "Just fine, but I just barely performed it in time!"
Nurse: "Was he in danger of dying?"
Doctor: "No, but in another two hours, the patient would have recovered without it!"

Two foreign doctors performed a female operation on a grouchy woman. Afterward, one told her husband, "You vife iz now impregnable."

"Oh, yes," commented the other doctor. "No question but vot she iz now inconceivable."

"I think what you both mean to say," replied her husband, "is that she is unbearable!"

Doctor: "You have nothing to worry about! You'll live to be eighty."
Patient: "I *am* eighty."
Doctor: "What did I tell you?"

Jack Benny once responded to an extravagant round of applause with the quip, "I don't deserve this, but then I have arthritis, and I don't think I deserve that either!"

Frustration—When your pacemaker gets a vaporlock.

Doctor: "I'm afraid that you are in serious condition. I will have to remove half your colon."
Patient: "Well, I guess it's better to have a semi-colon than a period!"

"Why do you take so many pills, Grandmother?" the little girl asked.

"Well," explained her grandmother, "I take the yellow ones for my liver, the pink ones for my stomach, and the black ones for my heart—and the red ones to direct traffic!"

I had to quit taking tranquilizers. I realized I was being nice to people I didn't even like.

Hearing

He finally invested in a hearing aid after becoming virtually deaf. It was one of those invisible hearing aids.

"Well, how do you like your new hearing aid?" asked his doctor.

"I like it great. I've heard sounds in the last few weeks that I didn't know existed."

"Well, how does your family like your hearing aid?"

"Oh, nobody in my family knows I have it yet. Am I having a great time! I've changed my will three times in the last two months!"

Wife: "My ear rings all the time and you don't seem to care about it."

Husband: "Oh, I do care about it."

Wife: "Well then, what do you suggest I do."

Husband: "Get an unlisted ear!"

A man and his wife both had hearing problems. "Look," he said, "when I say something to you, for goodness sake, show me that you heard me. Just grunt, say 'OK', 'Drop dead', 'I don't agree with you,' or just tell me that you heard me some way or another."

Her reply was rather unusual—"OK, I'll tell when I don't hear you."

They'd lived together for sixty years. He had never forgotten her birthday. However, as he was reading the morning newspaper over that extra cup of coffee, he noticed the date on the newspaper and remembered, "This is her birthday!"

He looked across the table to see if she had remembered. Evidently, she had forgotten, too. Sitting there for the next few minutes, their sixty years together passed through his mind. What a fine wife she had been through those many years of heartaches, struggles, joys, and victories. In his mind, she was as sweet and lovely as she was on the their wedding day. The only difference was that she had become a little hard of hearing over the years.

He leaned in her direction over his cup of coffee and yelled, "Wife, I'm proud of you!"

She sat straight up in her chair. Her eyes danced as she yelled, "That's nothing! I'm tired of you, too!"

Heaven & Hell

One Sunday our church bulletin announced that a sermon entitled, "There Is a Hell" was to be preached at an evangelistic conference. Then it added, "Some of our leaders will be there and bring back a first-hand report."

A salesman selling medical supplies dropped by the doctor's office one scorching hot afternoon and greeted the nurse. "And how is the Doc standing the heat?" he inquired.

"We don't really know," she stammered. "He's only been dead three days!"

A minister was visiting one of his ninety-year-old parishioners. "Soon," she said, "I'll be rocking in the bosom of Moses."

"No, dear," said the pastor. "The Bible says it's the bosom of Abraham."

"Well, at my age," she replied, "you

don't really care much about whose bosom it is!"

The ninety-two-year-old woman at a nursing home received a visit from one of her fellow church members. "How are you feeling?" the visitor asked.

"Oh," said the lady, "I'm just worried sick!"

"What are you worried about, dear?" her friend asked. "You look like you're in good health. They are taking care of you, aren't they?"

"Yes, they are taking good care of me."

"Are you in any pain?" she asked sympathetically.

"No, I have never had a pain in my life."

"Well, what are you worried about?" her friend queried.

She leaned back in her chair and slowly explained her major worry. "Every close friend I ever had has already died and gone on to heaven. I'm afraid they're all wondering where I went."

A sign on a bulletin board of a church down the street announced the topic for Sunday's sermon:

"Do You Know What Hell Is?"

Underneath, someone had scribbled, "Come and hear our organist!"

Holidays

During college days our neighbor in a next-door apartment gave their small boy a toy drum for Christmas. The kid beat on the contraption day and night. Finally, I grew weary of it. I gave the lad a new pocket knife and asked him if he knew what was inside the drum.

Santa's helpers are only subordinate clauses.

At Christmastime the Sunday School teacher rehearsed the boys for a play that was to be presented to the church during the worship hour. Four children, carrying huge, cut-out letters, were lined up to spell "S-T-A-R."

When the program began the audience began to chuckle. The four little performers marched out on the platform—in reverse order!

Husbands & Wives

My wife and I got married for better or worse. I couldn't do better and she couldn't do worse.

A husband who brags that he never made a mistake has a wife who made a big one!

My secret to a long, happy married life is simple. I try to treat my wife in such a way that if I died, it would take more than a hot water bottle to replace me.

Frankly, marriage is like twirling a baton, turning handsprings, or eating with chopsticks. It looks easy until you try it.

On our fortieth wedding anniversary my wife said warmly and affectionately, "Will you love me when I'm old and gray?"
"Well, of course," I assured her, "haven't I loved you through four other colors?"

Before I married Shirley, Dear,
  I was her pumpkin pie,
Her precious peach, her honey lamb,

the apple of her eye.
But after years of married life,
   this thought I pause to utter;
Those fancy names are gone, and now
   I'm just her bread and butter.

I'm not saying my wife is old, but she does remember when Heinz had only seven varieties and Howard Johnson boasted of two flavors.

One woman complained to her neighbor over the backyard fence about feeling lousy.

"What happened, did you wake up grouchy?"

"No, I just let him sleep in this morning."

My wife does not wish for jewels or furs,
Or lovely serenades at dawn.
She only wishes that I would put
The toothpaste cap back on!

My neighbor is perfectly happy. He has a wonderful home, a good job, and the best wife in the country. Who wouldn't be happy with a wife in the country!

Give my wife an inch—and the whole family goes on a diet.

I heard my wife telling the neighbor that I was a model husband. I felt pretty good until I looked up the word in the dictionary: "A model is a small imitation of the real thing."

Now she says, "Don't stand there with your fists doubled up at me in your pockets! Furthermore, when I want your opinion, I'll give it to you!"
But I just stand my ground, set my jaw, and give her a good listening to.

When I interviewed for a job, they asked how I'd feel about having a woman boss.
"Well," I replied, "I'd feel right at home."

My wife told the psychiatrist that I thought I was a refrigerator. "But it isn't so bad," she added, "except he leaves the door open and the light keeps me awake all night."

Husbands and wives need each other, but often find difficulty getting along. They've been likened to porcupines on a cold, winter night. The trick is staying close enough together to keep from freezing to death, and far enough apart to keep from sticking each other to death.
They are much like the swimming in-

structor who asked a little boy to explain the buddy system.

"It's somebody you drown with," he answered.

My wife and I were getting along fine until we got a waterbed. Ever since we've been drifting apart!

Insurance

Supervisor to agent: "I noticed here that you have written an insurance policy for a man who is ninety-five years of age."

Insurance agent: "Yes. What a tremendous deal!"

Supervisor: "What do you mean 'tremendous deal'? Do you realize how old that man is?"

Agent: "Yes, I realize how old he is. I checked the census reports. Do you realize how *few* people die after the age of ninety-five?"

The following are actual statements found on insurance forms where car drivers attempt to summarize the details of an accident in the fewest words possible.

"Coming home I drove into the wrong house and collided with a tree I don't have."

"The other car collided with mine without giving warning of its intentions."

"I thought my window was down, but I found out it was up when I put my head through it."

"I collided with a stationary truck coming the other way."

"A truck backed through my windshield into my wife's face."

"A pedestrian hit me and went under my car."

"The guy was all over the road. I had to swerve a number of times before I hit him."

"I pulled away from the side of the road, glanced at my mother-in-law, and headed over the embankment."

"In an attempt to kill a fly, I drove into a telephone pole."

"I had been shopping for plants all day and was on my way home. As I reached an intersection a hedge sprang up, obscuring my vision, and I did not see the other car."

"I had been driving for forty years when

I fell asleep at the wheel and had an accident."

"I was on my way to the doctor with rear-end trouble when my universal joint gave way causing me to have an accident."

"To avoid hitting the bumper of the car in front, I struck the pedestrian."

"As I approached the intersection a stop sign suddenly appeared in a place where no stop sign had ever appeared before. I was unable to stop in time to avoid the accident."

"My car was legally parked as it backed into the other vehicle."

"An invisible car came out of nowhere when it struck my car and vanished."

"I told the police that I was not injured, but on removing my hat, found that I had a fractured skull."

"I was sure the old fellow would never make it to the other side of the road when I struck him."

"The pedestrian had no idea which direction to run, so I ran over him."

"I saw a slow-moving, sad-faced old gentleman as he bounced off the roof of my car."

"The indirect cause of the accident was a little guy in a small car with a big mouth."

"I was thrown from my car as it left the road. I was later found in a ditch by some stray cows."

"The telephone pole was approaching. I was attempting to swerve out of its way when I struck the front end."

The insurance agent was surprised to find a couple in a retirement village with no insurance. In his effort to sell a policy to the husband, he said, "How in the world would your wife carry on if you should die!"

"Well," answered the husband, "I really don't care how she carries on after I die, just as long as she behaves herself as long as I'm alive."

Friends were trying to comfort the widow of a tugboat captain who had recently drowned. "Poor dear," said one, "I hope you were left with something."

"Oh," she replied, "I was left with an insurance policy that will give me over two-hundred thousand dollars."

"Imagine that," said a friend. "And he couldn't even read or write."

The widow looked up and said, "Or swim!"

An insurance agent was writing a policy for a cowboy. "Ever had an accident?" the agent asked.

"Nope," the cowboy replied. "But I've been bit by a rattlesnake and kicked by a few broncs."

"Don't you call those accidents?" the agent asked.

"Nope, the critters did it on purpose!"

Memory (Forgetfulness)

You're getting old when there's no question in your mind that there's no question in your mind.

Two elderly ladies were sitting on a porch rocking back and forth in rocking chairs. "Sally," said one, "do you ever think about the hereafter?"

As quick as a flash, Sally replied, "All the time! I go into a room and look around and

say, 'Now what was it I came in here after?' "

"Who Wrote Whom?"

Just a line to say I'm living,
    that I'm not among the dead.
Though I'm getting more forgetful
    and mixed up in the head.
I got used to my arthritis,
    to my dentures I'm resigned.
I can manage my bifocals,
    but I sure do miss my mind.
For sometimes I can't remember
    when I stand at the foot of the stairs,
If I must go up for something,
    or have I just come down from there.
And before the fridge so often,
    my poor mind is filled with doubt,
Have I just put food away, or
    have I come to take some out.
And there's time when it is dark
    with my nightcap on my head,
I don't know if I'm retiring, or
    just getting out of bed.
So, if it's my turn to write you,
    there's no need for getting sore,
I may think that I have written,
    and don't want to be a bore.
So, remember that I love you,
    and wish that you were near.
But now it's nearly mail time
    so must say good-bye, dear.

There I stand before the mailbox,
   with a face so very red.
Instead of mailing you my letter,
   I had opened it instead.

—Anonymous

Older patient: "Doc, I think I am becoming forgetful."

Doctor: "Sorry to hear that."

Patient: "What do you suggest I do, Doc?"

Doctor: "Pay me in advance!"

The older couple were sitting around the fireplace one evening. "Do you know what would taste real good before we go to bed?" she asked.

"No, what would you like?" her husband asked.

"Well, we don't really have any. You would have to walk down to the corner grocery store to get it."

"Well, just tell me what you want."

"I think I'd like some ice cream."

"What flavor," he asked.

"Vanilla would be fine, but you had better write it down. You know how bad your memory is."

"Oh, I can remember vanilla ice cream. Anything else?"

"Yeah," she said, "I think I'd like a little

chocolate syrup on it, but you had better write it down."

"Oh, I can remember; anything else?"

"Yeah, I believe I would like some nuts."

"That's vanilla ice cream, chocolate syrup, and nuts. I can remember!" he said as he walked out.

"You had better write it down," she said. "You're getting so forgetful these days."

Thirty minutes later he walked into the house with a pound of bacon. She opened the sack, looked in, and said, "I told you you're getting forgetful. Where are the *eggs?*"

I recently met a Texan with a bad case of amnesia—he couldn't remember the Alamo!

Three professors went to a railroad station. On the way they got into a deep philosophical conversation. Suddenly, the train started pulling out. Two of the professors scrambled aboard.

"It's good they got on that train in time," the porter said.

"Well, maybe," replied the professor left behind. "But they came down to see *me* off."

Memories

Times sure have changed. Today school systems spend a fortune soundproofing rooms with special kinds of expensive floors and ceilings. When I was a boy schools soundproofed me.

I was born at a very early age, at home, so I could be near my mother. I don't want to say I was an ugly baby, but the doctor took one look at me and made a citizen's arrest on my father.

I was six months old before I saw the light of day. My mother was nearsighted and kept diapering the wrong end.

I came from sturdy stock. My daddy lived to be ninety and never used glasses—he drank right out of the jug!

There were six kids in all. One day a stranger stopped my mother and asked, "Lady, are all those your kids, or are you on a picnic?"

"Mister," my mother sighed, "they're all mine, and believe me it's no picnic."

I grew up in a small town. Really small. It was so small they had to extend the city limits to install a phone booth. We had a beauty contest and no one won. It was so small we didn't even have a town drunk—we had to take turns.

Some folks had six rooms and a bath. We had four rooms and a path. It was what you might call a deep-seated tradition.

One of our neighbors, a farmer down the road, was rather prolific. He had ten kids. During the Fall season he took them to the fair to see a prize bull.

Approaching the ticket seller, the farmer said, "Mister, this here's my wife and ten kids. I'll give you five dollars to let us take a look at that bull."

The ticket seller, looking at him and then the ten kids, scratched his head. "Tell you what," he said, "I'll give you ten dollars if you'll let me go get that bull and let him take a look at you!"

My country cousin, Tom, went off to one of those big-city colleges. After he finished he returned to work on his dad's farm. He plowed the same, but when he got to the end of a row, instead of saying, "Whoa, haw, and gee," he said, "Halt, Rebecca, pivot and proceed!"

For Christmas dinner we always had plenty of chicken and dressing. My little sister said, "I don't like the chicken, but I like the bread he ate!"

I'll never forget the day I graduated from grammar school—I was so nervous I could hardly shave.

I must have lived close to the school. Everyday when I'd get home my mother would say, "Goodness, gracious, are you home already!"

I was always getting in trouble at school for things I didn't do—like arithmetic, history, biology, and so forth.

But the teachers kept asking me hard questions, like one asked me to define "space."

"I can't put it into words," I replied, "but I have it in my head."

My biology teacher assigned the class to type a 100-word theme on a frog. Boy, I thought I'd never get that blooming thing in the typewriter!

But my Dad was understanding when he saw my failing grade in geometry. "Don't worry about it, Son," he comforted me. "Don't nobody speak it much anymore, anyway! Besides," he concluded, "with grades like yours you couldn't be cheating!"

My teacher had no sense of humor and didn't think my answer to a test question was one bit funny: "This is one of those problems I'm content to leave with my elders until I'm old enough to turn it over to my children."

Mottoes

John D. Yeck is the founder of an organization which he calls, "The Let's Have Better Mottoes Association, Inc." Some of his funniest mottoes shared in his monthly newsletter are as follows:

FOOLS RUSH IN WHERE FOOLS HAVE BEEN BEFORE.

I'M SO COMPLETELY OPEN-MINDED ON THE ISSUE THAT I'LL EVEN LISTEN TO YOUR FANTASTICALLY STUPID, IDIOTIC OPINION.

TO AVOID DUPLICATION, MAKE THREE COPIES.

DO NOT DISTURB—GENIUS AT WERK.

IT'S CALLED "TAKE HOME" PAY BECAUSE YOU CAN'T AFFORD TO GO ANYWHERE ELSE WITH IT.

SUCCESS IS RELATIVE; THE GREAT-

ER THE SUCCESS, THE MORE RELA-
TIVES.

MY WORK IS SO SECRET EVEN I
DON'T KNOW WHAT I'M DOING.

ANYONE CAN BE A WINNER—UN-
LESS, OF COURSE, THERE'S A SECOND
ENTRY.

IT'S BETTER TO HAVE LOAFED AND
LOST THAN NEVER TO HAVE LOAFED
AT ALL.

THE SLOWER YOU WORK, THE
FEWER MISTEAKS YOU MAKE.

FOR EVERY VISION THERE IS AN
EQUAL AND OPPOSITE REVISION.

IF MURPHY'S LAW CAN GO
WRONG, IT WILL.

YOU CAN SAY ANYTHING YOU
PLEASE AROUND HERE BUT SOME
THINGS ONLY ONCE.

IF AT FIRST YOU SUCCEED, TRY TO
HIDE YOUR ASTONISHMENT.

YOU MUST HAVE LEARNED FROM
OTHERS' MISTAKES. YOU HAVEN'T
HAD TIME TO THINK ALL THOSE UP
YOURSELF.

YOUR VISIT IS THE HIGHLIGHT OF

MY DAY; SO YOU KNOW WHAT KIND OF DAY I'VE HAD.

IF YOU LOOK LIKE YOUR PASSPORT PICTURE, YOU PROBABLY NEED THE TRIP.

NEVER DO YOUR BEST; IT LEAVES NO ROOM FOR IMPROVEMENT.

NEVER BE REDUNTANT—NEVER, NEVER, NEVER, NEVER.

I *LIKE* CRITICISM. JUST KEEP IT POSITIVE AND FLATTERING.

INDECISION MAY OR MAY NOT BE THE PROBLEM HERE.

IT'S OK TO LET YOUR MIND GO BLANK, BUT PLEASE TURN OFF THE SOUND.

I TOLERATE ALL OPINIONS—EVEN STUPID ONES LIKE YOURS.

PEOPLE CLAIM I'M INDECISIVE BUT I'M NOT SO SURE.

EXPERIENCE IS WHAT TELLS YOU YOU'VE MADE A MISTAKE. . . AGAIN.

I AM *NOT* ARBITRARY AND I WON'T DISCUSS IT FURTHER.

I'M GOING TO BECOME MORE AS-

SERTIVE IF IT'S 100 PERCENT OK WITH YOU.

PLEASE DON'T ARGUE. I'VE CHANGED MY MIND ALREADY.

WORRY KILLS MORE PEOPLE THAN WORK BECAUSE MORE PEOPLE WORRY THAN WORK.

I NEVER MAKE A MISTAKE BUT I'M GETTING TIRED OF DOING NOTHING.

I RESPECT YOUR OPINION BUT I'D RESPECT IT EVEN MORE IF YOU'D KEEP IT TO YOURSELF.

IF AT FIRST YOU DON'T SUCCEED . . . LOOK IN THE WASTEBASKET FOR THE DIRECTIONS.

PROCRASTINATION AVOIDS BORE-DOM—THERE'S ALWAYS SOMETHING LEFT TO DO.

Optimism (Pessimism)

A Protestant felt too guilty about his sin of stealing to tell his own pastor, so he went to a Catholic priest to confess.

"I have been stealing lumber from the

local lumberyard for ten years," the man confided to the priest.

"Well, my Son," said the sympathetic priest, "we must talk about restitution."

"Anything you say!"

"How much lumber do you suppose you have stolen through the years? Five hundred dollars worth? A thousand dollars worth? Two thousand dollars worth?"

"Oh, more than that," answered the thief.

"Do you want to make a Novena?" the priest asked.

The fellow cocked his head and said, "If you've got the plans for it, I've got the lumber!"

Pets

Did you hear about the hummingbird and door bell that fell in love, got married, and had a little humdinger?

Our neighbor looked out the front window and saw her small son romping up the walk carrying a little spotted puppy. She met him at the door and commanded, "You take that puppy right back where you got him and bring your baby sister home!"

A man went in to buy a talking parrot at the pet shop. He was promptly sold a parrot in a cage for a sizable amount of money.

"Are you sure this parrot will talk?" the man asked.

The pet shop owner said, "No doubt about it. He'll be talking within a day or so."

The man took the parrot home and stayed up all night watching it and listening for it to talk, but he said nothing.

The next day he went back to the pet shop and said, "I stayed up all night watching that parrot and he didn't say a word."

"Well, what did he do when he ran up and down that little ladder?"

"Ladder? The cage you sold me didn't have a ladder."

"Well, I have them here. They are ten dollars."

"Then give me a ladder," the man said and left.

He came back the next day and announced that he had spent the whole night watching and waiting for his bird to talk as it ran up and down the ladder.

"Well," the pet shop owner said, "they

usually talk after they look into that little mirror."

"Little mirror?" the man asked. "My cage doesn't have a little mirror."

"I sell them here for five dollars."

So the man bought a mirror and took it home. He came back the next day and announced, "I've been up three days and nights watching that stupid bird and he hasn't said a word."

"Well," the pet shop owner said, "they usually talk after they get a little exercise running up and down that ladder. When they look into the mirror they think it is another bird and immediately begin to talk. What does he do when he pecks on the bell?"

"The bell? My cage doesn't have a bell!"

"They are three dollars."

The man purchased a bell and left. He came back the next day and announced that the bird hadn't said a word.

"Well, I can't understand that," the pet shop owner said. "They usually run up and down the ladder, look in the mirror, peck that little bell, and when they set on that swing in the top of the cage, they jabber day and night."

"Swing at the top of the cage?" the man screamed. "My cage doesn't have a swing! How much?"

"They're just two dollars."

The man went home with his swing and didn't return for a couple of days. The pet shop owner looked up and saw him coming into his shop despondent and exhausted.

"I've been up seven days and nights," the man said, "watching that little bird, and finally he said something."

"What did he say?" the pet shop owner said.

"Well, last night all night long he ran up and down that ladder, looked in that mirror, pecked on that bell, got on that swing to swing back and forth in the cage. Finally, early this morning he turned upside down on the swing and dropped to the bottom of the cage on his back. I leaned over and looked in the cage. The parrot looked up at me and spoke his first words."

"What did he say?" asked the pet shop owner.

"Don't they sell birdseed at that pet shop?"

Did you hear about the little boy who practiced his violin. As he scratched away on the instrument the hound dog howled dismally along with the boy's playing.

Finally, in desperation, his mother screamed at her son, "I can't stand it anymore! Can't you play something the dog doesn't know!"

A man and his wife were planning a vacation in Florida, but they didn't know what to do with their dog. So the husband wrote the hotel manager and asked if dogs were allowed. He promptly answered:

"Dear Sir:
"I've been in the hotel business for thirty years and I've never had to call the police to eject a disorderly dog; never had a dog set fire to a bed with a cigarette; never found a hotel towel in a dog's suitcase; and never had a dog leave a glass ring on the top of the dresser. Your dog is welcome.
        Signed: the Manager
"P.S. If your dog will vouch for you, you can come along, too."

Politics (Government)

If the world keeps getting smaller, how come it costs more to run it?

If the country is going to the dogs, maybe

it's because the congressmen haven't been to obedience school.

He took his Social Security check down to the bank to deposit it. As he stood and waited in the long line, he inadvertantly began to nervously fold and unfold his check.

It finally came his turn at the teller's window. As he handed the teller a ruffled government check she said, "Sir, can't you read this check? It says, 'Do not fold, spindle, or mutilate.' "

"So?" replied the customer.

"Well," said the teller, "You shouldn't do that. The government doesn't like it."

Looking her straight in the eye he replied, "Well, the government does a lot of things I don't like, too!"

Two residents of a retirement village were discussing the two candidates for mayor in the city. "The only good thing about it," said one, "is that only one of them will be elected."

A local politician was visiting a nursing home. "Well," one little old lady replied to the persistant politician, "you're my second choice."

"Oh, I'm honored by that, Madam, but may I ask, who is your first choice?"

"Oh," she replied casually, "anybody else who is running for the same office!"

An election year is when the air is filled with speeches and vice versa.

I listened to one of those politicians waxing eloquent one day.

"If I'm elected," he promised, "I'll get rid of socialism, communism, and anarchism . . ."

"Yeah," interrupted an old man from the back of the room, "and let's throw out rheumatism, too!"

The reason so many politicians are anxious to get reelected is they are afraid to try to make a living back home under the laws they passed in Washington.

Have you noticed that politicians' promises of yesterday are the taxes of today?

Some politicians' minds are like concrete —thoroughly mixed and permanently set.

Don't waste your money, you've got a government to support. But sometimes I wonder if they use the tax money wisely. For instance, they spend fifty thousand dollars for a school bus to keep kids from walking, then spend half-a-million dollars for a gym so they can get exercise.

Recreation

Nothing increases your golf score like a witness.

My doctor gives me lots of advice. Recently he said, "The best thing for you is to give up golf, tennis, and keep earlier hours."

Aw, Doc," I replied, "I don't deserve the best. What's second best?"

The recreation director for a certain retirement village decided to revive some of the dances of the olden days.

It was "Twist" night and the senior adults were "cutting the rug." Two dogs walked by the recreation room and looked in. One said, "What in the world are they doing in there?"

The other dog said, "I don't know, but if we did it they would medicate us!"

Old fishermen never die—they just smell that way!

The fisherman watched a weatherbeaten old guide in the adjoining boat carefully cut a fishing line partway through a few inches above the brightly colored lure.

"Why are you doing that?" he asked.

"I'm fixing to take an amateur out pretty soon," the old fisherman explained. "He'll likely snag a fair-sized fish right off. When he goes to lift him into the boat the line will break. That feller will tell all his friends about the big one that got away." The old man looked about slyly, then added, "What's more, he'll come back here every summer for the rest of his life trying to catch that big one."

On fishing trips we never face famine.
We always take along a can of salmon.

On a fishing trip I was outfitted in complete fishing regalia, including a hat with my fishing license prominently displayed on its side.

After fishing all day with no luck, my son said to me, "Dad, why don't you turn your hat around so the fish can see your license?"

Remarriage

Ben and Mary had lived together as a married couple for over sixty years. On one occasion she went to her beautician with this request, "Make me look like Ben's second wife."

One couple was so old when they married that they applied to Medicare for payments on their honeymoon.

The groundskeeper at the cemetery heard the cries of an elderly man as he lay across the grave. He was crying, "Why did you die, oh, why did you die?"

"Was that your wife?" he asked.

"No, no, it wasn't my wife. Oh, why did you die? Why did you die?"

"Was it a friend of yours?"

"No, no, I never knew the person. Oh, why did you die? Why did you die?"

"It was not a member of your family?"

"No, it was not a member of my family. Oh, why did you die? Why did you die?"

"Who, Sir, then is buried in that grave?"

"My wife's first husband."

George had been happily married for over forty years. Upon his wife's death he became depressed and moved into a nursing home.

One day it occurred to him, *Why in the world am I so depressed? Why don't I get out of this place and live again? I'm sure my wife would want me to marry again if I could find the right kind of woman.*

George changed everything about himself. He got a toupee for his balding head. He went on a diet and lost thirty pounds. He bought some bright clothes and a gold neckchain. He even bought a bright red convertible sports car. George was a new man. At a church social, he met a widow about twenty years younger than he. It was a whirlwind courtship and within a few weeks they were planning marriage. George changed his whole life-style and found a new mate!

After the wedding, George and his new bridge were driving to their honeymoon cottage with the top down on his red convertible. They ran into a terrible storm. George stopped the car, put up the top on the convertible, and got out to see how it looked. A bolt of lightning struck him. George soon stood in the presence of the Lord.

"Why Lord? Why me, why now?" asked George.

The Lord replied, "Why George, I didn't even recognize you!"

The older man knelt before his new and exciting love. "I have two questions to ask you," he said.

"Yes, yes," was the enthusiastic response.

"Will you marry me?"

"Oh, yes. I was waiting for you to ask me! Now what is your second question?"

"Will you help me up?"

My bachelor neighbor sneaked up behind an older woman, covered her eyes with his hands, and said, "I'm going to kiss you if you can't tell me who I am in three guesses."

"George Washington! Thomas Jefferson! Abraham Lincoln!" she answered quickly.

I should have known better when I proposed to her and asked, "Darling, do you think you can live on what I make?"

"Sure," she replied, "but I don't know what you're going to live on."

Retirement

The worst thing about retirement is having to drink coffee on your own time.

We could all retire comfortably if we could sell our experience for what it cost us.

A young preacher was serving as a volunteer chaplain at a large nursing home. He had never performed a wedding and upon asking an older preacher in town what to do in case he forgot during the wedding ceremony, he was advised, "Just start quoting Scripture until something comes to you."

Soon the young preacher was called upon to perform the wedding ceremony for a widow and widower in the nursing home. Sure enough, right in the middle of the ceremony he forgot what to say next. So, thinking of the advice of the older preacher, he started quoting Scripture. But the only Scripture he could remember was, "Father, forgive them for they know not what they do!"

Overheard in a retirement village:

First widow: "They say he married her because her first husband left her a million dollars."

Second widow: "Oh, I don't think he's that kind of a fellow. I think he would have married her regardless of who left her the million dollars."

An elderly country-western singer finally announced his retirement. Reason? His adenoids cleared up!

Two men were discussing the hobbies and crafts offered at the retirement village in which they and their wives were living. "Is your wife an active member of the sewing circle?" asked one man.

"No," the other man shook his head, "she just sits there and sews!"

Several years after his retirement, Joe decided to go back down to the office and see how things were going. Just to see how well he was remembered, he decided to go in and ask for himself.

"Can I speak to Joe Smith?" he asked a bright young secretary in the front office.

"Oh," she said, "Joe Smith doesn't work here anymore."

"Well," he said, "let me speak to the man who filled his vacancy."

"Well," the secretary said, "Joe didn't leave a vacancy!"

To some men in retirement, the whole point of the day is to get the figure on the golf score down as low as the one on the Social Security check.

Smoking

A tobacco company sent my cousin several packages of cigarettes with the explanation: "We are sending you some of our finest cigarettes. We hope you enjoy them and will want more."

After several months the tobacco company received this reply from my cousin. "I got your cigarettes and soaked them in a quart of water which I sprayed on my bug-infested rosebushes. Every bug died! The cigarettes are sure good poison. Please send me some more next spring in case any bugs survived."

Did you hear about the fanatic who hated cigarettes? He went around stomping every one he saw. And a few years later he died of foot cancer.

A tobacco company had heard that the oldest citizen of a certain village had been smoking their product for over fifty years. They dispatched a public-relations man to the retirement village to interview him.

"Sir," the P.R. man said, "we are prepared to fly you to New York City to appear on an early morning television show to give a testimonial about our tobacco company."

"Can't do it!" replied the seasoned smoker.

"You can't do it?" asked the P.R. man. "Don't you want a free plane ticket to New York?"

"Yep, I'd like to go to New York, but I can't do it."

"Well, Sir," said the P.R. man, "we're prepared to put you up in one of the nicest hotels in New York City for at least three nights. Wouldn't that be wonderful?"

"Yep, it would be wonderful, but I can't do it!"

"Why can't you do it?" screamed the P.R. man.

"Well, young fellow," he said, "I can't fly to New York City and appear on that morning television show to give a testimonial about your tobacco because I don't stop coughing until noon!"

Speaking

Oratory is the art of making sounds deep within the chest sound like important messages from the heart.

I was a promising speaker in college—they made me promise never to try it again.

I almost quit speaking on account of my throat—audiences kept threatening to cut it!

Actually, at my last speaking engagement, I drew a line three blocks long. Then some smart aleck took my chalk away from me!

I know I don't have any talent for speaking, but now I've become so famous at it, I can't give it up.

I always start speaking at 7 PM sharp and end at 8 PM dull.

Not long ago on a speaking engagement, I noticed a sign near the speaker's platform (for the benefit of people taking flash pictures) that read:

"Do not photograph the speaker while he is addressing the audience. Shoot him as he leaves the platform."

Once I was hurrying to the auditorium to make a speech when a reporter stopped me and asked me some deep philosophical question.

"Don't bother me now," I snapped, "I've got to make a speech and this is no time to think!"

My wife is really the speaker in the family. She speaks 150 words a minute with gusts up to 180.

She believes in the discipline of silence, and can talk hours about it.

That's why they call it the "mother tongue"—the father seldom ever gets to use it.

My wife went to the doctor. He examined her and said, "You're okay, you only need more rest."

"But look at my tongue!" she insisted.

"Yeah!" the doctor replied. "It needs rest, too."

Our daughter is the picture of her father and the soundtrack of her mother.

One of my kinfolk donated a loudspeaker to our church in memory of his wife.

Special Occasions

They had lived together in the backwoods for over fifty years. To celebrate their fiftieth anniversary, he took her to a large city and they checked into a plush hotel.

She said to the bellman, "We refuse to settle for such a small room. No windows, no bed, no fan," she complained.

"But, Madam!"

"Don't 'But, Madam' me," she continued. "You can't treat us like we're a couple of fools just because we don't travel much, and we've never been to the big city, and never spent the night at a hotel. I'm going to complain to the manager."

"Madam," the bellman said, "this isn't your room; this is the elevator!"

The nicest gift is always something you made yourself . . . like money.

She was ninety years of age. Her little house was filled with knick-knacks and what-nots people had given her for her birthday.

A friend asked, "And what do you want for your ninetieth birthday?"

"Give me a kiss," she answered, "so I won't have to dust it!"

You will always stay young if you live honestly, sleep sufficiently, eat slowly, work industriously, and fib about your age.

My wife refuses to have candles on her birthday cake. She said she was in no mood to make light of her age.

It's just as well. If we put all those candles on the cake it would be a fire hazard.

Sports

A five-year-old girl had gone fishing with her grandfather. After an hour or so her grandfather asked her, "Are you having any luck?"

She replied indignantly, "No, I don't think my worm is really trying."

At every ball game there are a few men who can play every position superbly without an error. Now if we can just get them to put down their hot dogs and climb down from the bleachers.

My wife complains about my playing golf.

"You never think of anything but golf," she declared. "Why, I'll bet you don't even remember the day we got married."

"Of course, I do, Honey," I insisted. "It was the day I sank that forty-foot putt."

They had just settled in to a retirement village. One man said to the other, "I got some new golf clubs for my wife."

Happily, the other man replied, "Wow! That's great! I wish I could make a trade like that."

Overheard in the clubhouse of a retirement village: "It's not that I cheat," the golfer explained, "it's just that I play golf for my health and a low score makes me feel better!"

The best golfer at a retirement village was an eighty-year-old man. He could hit the ball two-hundred-and-fifty yards every time. However, he was losing his eyesight and couldn't follow the trajectory of his ball.

He met another eighty-year-old friend who was not as good a golfer but had twenty-twenty vision. "I have a great idea," he exclaimed. "Let's play golf together. You can see well enough to tell where my ball lands."

On their first day out, the big knocker stepped up to the ball and hit it two-hundred-and-seventy-five yards. The other man replied, "I see it, I see it, I see it."

"Where did it go?" asked the long hitter.

The other man turned to him with a blank stare and said, "I forgot!"

I love baseball-maybe too much. Once I went to a psychiatrist. "What's the matter?" he asked.

"It's baseball," I explained. "I always dream about baseball—nothing but baseball!"

"Don't you ever dream about girls?" the doctor asked.

"Oh, no! Never!" I replied. "I'd lose my turn at bat!"

My wife complains about me watching so much baseball on television. I really don't know why she complains; we can always talk on the days the games are rained out.

If it hadn't been for baseball, I would never have learned to diaper my babies. An old player, father of eight, explained it in terms I could understand:

"Spread the diaper in the position of a baseball diamond, with you at the bat. Then, fold second base down to home plate and set the baby on the pitcher's mound. Put first base and third base together and pin. In case of rain you gotta start all over again!"

During college I played awhile, that is, until we played William and Mary. They beat the daylights out of us. We never played William again—just Mary!

I like to go to football games, but they always seat me between the hot-dog peddler and his best customer. Or they place me beside a silly spectator who thinks he's got four quarters in which to finish a fifth.

Once our boys' team played a girls' team in football. I don't know what the score was, but when the game was over our team had been penalized a mile behind the goal line for holding.

Have you noticed that every Spring

farmers and golfers begin their plowing at the same time.

Golfers say they shoot their age. It's more like their weight, if you ask me.

I like the definition of golf by one man who said, "It is an ineffectual endeavor to put an insignificant pellet into an obscure hole with an inadequate instrument."

It doesn't seem fair. By the time a person can afford to lose a golf ball, he can't hit it that far.

Golf is a lot like taxes—you drive hard to get to the green and then wind up in the hole.

Success

Old Age—Just when you're successful enough to sleep late, you're so old you always wake up early.

Do you know the difference between a Yuppie and a Guppie?

1. *Definition:* A Yuppie is a Young Urban Professional. A Guppie is a Graying Urban Procrastinator.

2. *Commitment:* a Yuppie is interested in being committed to one mate. A Guppie is trying to find ways to commit his or her mate.

The secret of success is to always have more answers than people have questions.

It is much better to say, "We're moving in cycles," than "We're running around in circles."

A man whispered to his wife as they arrived at a party, "Your left stocking seam is crooked."

She made adjustment without being noticed by anyone. Then she whispered to him, "Is my right seam alright?"

"Sure," he replied. "It's seamless."

Once an escaped convict headed for our small town. The big-city police were hot on his trail and called our local sheriff. The city police sent the sheriff a dozen pictures of the wanted man: profile, full face, standing, sitting, and in various poses.

Within twenty-four hours our super sheriff called the city police back. "I've caught eleven of those crooks," he boasted, "and I'll get the other one before morning!"

The Bible teaches us importunity—to keep on asking. My little daughter came here already knowing that. One long, tiring day, my wife and I finally got her to bed, said our prayers, tucked her in, turned off the lights, and retreated to the family room to watch some uninterrupted television.

Hardly had we settled down when we heard our small daughter's voice cry, "Daddy! I want a drink of water."

"You've had a drink of water," I replied. "Now go to sleep."

After a couple of minutes again came the plaintive pleas, "Daddy! I need a drink of water."

"No!" I said in a stern voice, "and if you ask me one more time, I'll come in there and spank you."

A brief silence followed. Then her wee voice wailed, "Daddy, when you come in here to spank me, would you bring me a drink of water?"

Don't worry too much about success. Even if you get it your wife will take the credit and the government will take the cash.

Besides, success is something that always

comes faster to the man your wife almost married.

When you make your mark in the world, somebody will come along with an eraser.

A successful person is one who wears last year's clothes, drives this year's car, and lives on next year's income.

If you're going to climb higher, you've got to grab the branches, not the blossoms.

There's plenty of room at the top, but there's no room to sit down.

The world isn't interested in the storm you encountered, but only if you brought in the ship.

Have you ever noticed that people who complain about the way the ball bounces are usually the ones who dropped it?

Isn't it strange that people who are successful and have what they want are fond of telling unsuccessful people who don't have what they want that they really don't want it.

Grandma devised a foolproof, no-cost,

security system. She hung a key by a cord to the front doorknob. Naturally, the key didn't fit, but by the time the intruder realized the key wouldn't work, Grandma was out the backdoor and around the house holding a shotgun on the culprit.

Survival (Determination)

An ancient myth teaches that at creation, the dog, the horse, the monkey, and human beings were given forty years each to live on this earth. The dog, the horse, and the monkey said, "We don't need all that time to live." So, they each gave man ten years of their allotted forty years.

Now you know why man leads a dog's life between forty and fifty, works like a horse between fifty and sixty, and after that just monkeys around.

"To The Class of '42"

Attention, 1942 classmates!
We are survivors!

It is said that there are three ages of man:
(1) youth, (2) middle, and (3) "You haven't

changed a bit!" But change is the name of the game. Consider:

We were before television, before penicillin, before polio shots, frozen foods, Xerox, contact lenses, Frisbees and the Pill. We were before radar, credit cards, split atoms, laser beams, and ball-point pens. We were before pantyhose, dishwashers, clothes dryers, electric blankets, and automatic shift. We got married first and then lived together. How quaint can you be!

In our time closets were for clothes, not for "coming out of." Bunnies were small rabbits and rabbits were not Volkswagens. We thought a deep cleavage was something a butcher did. Designer jeans were scheming girls named Jean or Jeanne, and having a meaningful relationship meant getting along well with your cousin. We thought fast food was what you ate during Lent, and Outer Space was the balcony at the local theater. We were before househusbands, gay rights, computer dating, dual careers, and commuter marriages. We were before day-care centers, group therapy, and nursing homes. We never heard of FM radio, computer chips, tape decks, electric typewriters, artificial hearts, word processors, yogurt, and guys wearing earrings. We'd have thought ERA and JFK, DOT and LUD were lovers' initials lettered on a school jacket or in a slam book.

We hit the scene when there were 5-

and-10 cent stores where you bought things for five and ten cents. The ice-cream store sold ice-cream cones for a nickel or a dime. For one nickel you could make a phone call, buy a Coke or enough stamps to mail one letter and two postcards, and mail was delivered twice a day. You could buy a new Chevy coupe for $590, but who could afford one? And a pity, too, because gas was only 10 cents a gallon!

In our day cigarette smoking was fashionable, Grass was mowed, Coke was a cold drink at the corner drug store, and Pot was something you cooked in. Break dancing was something Charlie Henderson played for in the gym at the lunch period. Rock music was a Grandma's lullaby, and Aids were helpers in the cafeteria.

"It was the best of times; it was the worst of times," wrote Charles Dickens in *A Tale of Two Cities.*

We were certainly not before the difference between the sexes was discovered, but we were surely before the sex change. We made do with what we had. And we were the last generation that was so dumb as to think you needed a husband to have a baby.

But . . . we survived!

—Anonymous

Television

The difference between watching television and dying is that, with television, other people's lives flash before your eyes.

Television is still in its infancy. That's why we have to get up and change it so often.

The man and his wife from the backwoods came to town. They watched their first automatic washing machine with a round glass door toss and tumble the clothes. Finally the old man turned to his wife and said, "Well, Old Woman, if that's television, they can have it!"

The television salesman gave a man and his wife a demonstration of how to use a remote-controlled set. He hooked it up in their living room, took the remote-control transmitter a block down the street, and switched channels without difficulty.

But the wife didn't like it. She got tired of walking a block away every time she wanted to change channels.

Who said opportunity only knocks once? Television is giving us a second chance to see old movies we couldn't afford to see twenty years ago.

A commercial traveler these days is a person who goes to the refrigerator during the sponsor's message.

I bought a used television set that had had only one owner—a little old lady with weak eyes.

Television is called a medium because so much of it is neither rare nor well done.

Sometimes television programs are so bad I'm tempted to dredge the channel.

Television has increased the cost of living. When I was a boy I could see a western for twenty-five cents. Today it costs three-hundred dollars for a VCR to watch the same western.

I really don't mind my wife serving TV dinners, but here lately she's started serving reruns in the summer.

Some folks think television selling is new. Not so. It's actually the same form of selling that was common in the patent-medicine shows during my youth.

The medicine man would put a couple of song-and-dance people on a platform and when a crowd gathered he came out and sold his snake oil.

Television has only upgraded the song-and-dance people and increased the cost of the snake oil.

Time

By the time you finally stop and smell the roses, somebody's just spread out the fertilizer.

"Mrs. Bryan, how often does this horrible pain strike you?" inquired the doctor.

"Every five minutes, Doctor," replied the patient.

"And how long does it last?" asked Dr. Mort.

"Oh," replied Mrs. Bryan, "at least thirty minutes!"

My doctor once mentioned that he rarely attended a patient's funeral.

"Of course not," my wife chattered. "If

you tried, it wouldn't leave you time for anything else."

When guests have declared they must be going,
And my vision is getting blurry,
Why do I say (to my own dismay)
So convincingly, "What's your hurry?"

My wife is the world's worst at getting instructions mixed-up. For instance, when we were married, she bought one of those fancy, electric coffee makers. It had all kinds of gadgets on it.

The salesman carefully explained how the timer worked. "You plug it in, set the timer, go back to bed, and when you get up, the coffee is ready."

A couple of weeks later my wife was back in the store and the salesman asked her how she liked her new coffee maker.

"Great!" she replied, "But there's one thing I don't understand. Why do I have to go to bed every time I want to make a pot of coffee?"

Travel

Two women were talking: "I was chatting with your husband the other day and he tells me that you aren't going to Europe this summer."

"No," the other woman replied, "That was last year. This year we aren't going to Hawaii."

He was up in years before he ever had the opportunity to go to an airport. He had never seen an escalator. He stood in amazement watching the escalator go up and come down. Then, he noticed a whole busload of ladies from a local retirement village get on the escalator going down.

As he stood there watching the escalator come back up, it was filled with a group of young college coeds coming home for the holidays.

He said to himself, *I'm going to go right home now and get Ma and put her on this machine!*

A group of ladies from a retirement village loaded onto the bus to observe a local art exhibit. The artist himself was present to explain his paintings.

One lady walked up to an abstract painting and asked the artist, "What in the world is that supposed to be?"

Patiently, the artist said condescendingly, "Well, my dear lady, that's supposed to be a mother and her child."

"Well, why isn't it?" asked the art critic.

A plane full of retirees headed for Florida was gripped with fear when the pilot announced, "Two of our engines are on fire; we are flying through a heavy fog, and it has eliminated all our visibility."

The passengers were numb with fear, except for one—a retired minister. "Now, now, keep calm," he said. "Let's all bow our heads and pray."

Immediately, they bowed their heads to pray—except one man. "Why aren't you bowing your head to pray?" the minister asked.

"I don't know how to pray," replied the passenger.

"Well, just do something religious!" instructed the minister.

The man got up and passed his hat down the aisle, taking an offering.

A fellow was traveling out West. Suddenly, he was surrounded by Indians.

"It was terrible," he said to a sympathetic listener. "Indians to the right. Indians to the left. Everywhere I looked, there were Indians."

"What did you do?" someone asked.

"What could I do?" the fellow said. "I bought a blanket!"

A lady was aboard a ship during a terrible storm. She had undressed for bed when suddenly she was overcome by seasickness. In a panic, she rushed out into the corridor and headed for the bathroom.

Colliding with a man, she realized she had very little clothing on. Horrified, she let out a shriek.

"Lady," the bewildered man replied, also suffering from seasickness, "don't let it bother you. I'll never live to tell anybody!"

Remember riding in a car in the 30's and 40's reading the Burma Shave signs? The jingles on successive signs was a delight.

Within this vale
of toil and sin
Your head grows bald
but not your chin.

She kissed the hairbrush

by mistake.
She thought it was
her husband Jake.

I proposed to Ida;
Ida refused.
I'da won Ida if I'da used
Burma Shave.

They missed the turn;
Car was whizz'n.
Fault was her'n;
Funeral his'n.

Does your husband misbehave,
grunt and grumble, pant and rave?
Shoot the brute some Burma Shave.

Unclassified

There is one thing that most of us do better than anyone else—read our own handwriting.

Some people have their feet planted firmly on the ground . . . and others just move like it.

I heard of one cowboy that was so tough, he carried two guitars!

An eight-year-old boy wrote a composition about his father:

"He can climb the highest mountain or swim the biggest ocean. He can fly the fastest plane and fight the strongest tiger. My father can do anything. But most of the time he just carries out the garbage!"

Several years ago a friend was in trouble and I helped him out.

"I won't forget you," he promised. He didn't. He's in trouble again and he just called me.

Our house is a bungalow—the carpenters bungled the job, and we still owe for it.

I read in the newspaper about a man in Connecticut who was arrested for stealing a chicken from a market. He claimed the chicken flew under his coat. But the police doubted his story since the chicken was frozen.

The other day a young girl rang the doorbell and tried to sell me a ticket to a band concert.

"Sorry," I quickly replied, "I can't make it, but my spirit will be there with you."

"Good!" she replied. "I have two-dollar-,

three-dollar-, and five-dollar tickets. Where would your spirit like to sit?"

A little boy came home with a note from his teacher pinned to his jacket:

"Dear Parents:

"If you'll promise not to believe everything your child tells you that happens at school, I'll promise not to believe everything your child tells me happens at home."

I applied for a seat on the next flight to the moon. But the agent said, "Sorry, all flights to the moon have been cancelled. The moon is full right now."

Once a Texan visited in Australia. He told the folks down under how much bigger and better things were in Texas. Suddenly a kangaroo jumped in front of him.

"What in tarnation was that?" the startled Texan asked.

"You mean you don't have grasshoppers in Texas?" an Australian calmly replied.

Vacations

Vacation—a trip that puts you in the pink —and leaves you in the red.

Sunburn—Getting what you basked for.

A man is really getting smart when he realizes that vacations are disguised shopping sprees.

When you go on vacation with a car full of children, pets, toys, and suitcases, how can they call it "getting away from it all"?

A man and his wife were on vacation, and in a remote area found a little "greasy spoon" restaurant.

"We'll each have two eggs, toast and a cup of coffee," the man said to the waitress. "And, by the way, we'd like a few kind words."

The waitress promptly brought the order to the couple and walked away.

"What about our kind words?" the man asked.

The waitress leaned over and whispered in his ear, "Don't eat those eggs!"

A friend of mine went to Florida for his health. While there, he suddenly died. His body was shipped back home for burial. As friends viewed the body one said, "Doesn't he look wonderful!"

"Yes," replied another, "those two weeks in Florida did him a world of good."

I love taking vacation home movies so I can get back and find out what a wonderful time I had.

When vacations are over you often find,
As you give it a backward look,
You could have made out with half the clothes,
and twice the money you took.

Little bankroll ere we part,
Let me hug you to my heart;
All the year I've clung to you—
I've been faithful, you've been true!
Little bankroll, in a day,
You and I will start away
To a good vacation spot—
I'll come back, but you will not.

One summer I didn't go on vacation, but

I got the same effect by tipping every third person I met.

Actually, the reason we stayed home this year is because we took a pay-later vacation last year.

We couldn't afford a winter vacation either, but we did manage to save enough to turn the thermostat up for a weekend.

Weather

The weather is sometimes unpleasant. I remember one year so bad that it lasted thirteen months.

Don't you just hate muggy days? Everything that's supposed to stick together comes apart, and everything that's supposed to come apart sticks together.

I can just see it now: two cavemen huddled close to their fire. Outside it's raining, sleeting, thundering, and storming. One grumbles to the other, "You know, we never had this crazy weather before they started using bows and arrows!"

Our local weatherman has a way of

putting things. Last winter he reported it was "Still and clear . . . still snowing and clear up to your knees!"

One day he read the weather bulletin that called for fog. Looking out the window he saw it was raining. So he added, "But the fog is presently running down the gutters!"

Many a day I've had to shovel six inches of "partly cloudy" off my walk.

Widows (Widowers)

Just give me a man with a million or two,
Or one that is handsome would happily do.
A dashing young fellow is swell any day,
Or one who is famous will suit me okay.
But if the man shortage gets any worse,
Just go back to the first line of this verse.

A woman brought an old picture of her dead husband, wearing a hat, to the photographer. She wanted to know if the photographer could remove the hat from the picture. He assured her he could and asked her what side of his head he parted his hair on.

"I forgot," she said. "But you can see that for yourself when you take off his hat."

Soon after her husband died, she decided it was time for her to learn to drive a car. On her first trip to town, she drove right through a red light. "Don't you know what that sign means?" asked an angry policeman. "It means 'Stop'!" he explained.

"Oh, I'm so sorry, Officer," the elderly widow said.

"Haven't you ever driven before?" he asked.

"Well, yes and no."

" 'Yes and no.' What kind of answer is that?"

"Well, I have driven before, but this is the first time I've driven from the front seat!"

After performing the second marriage for an elderly widow and widower, the pastor remarked to his wife, "I'm afraid their marriage will not be particularly happy."

"Why not, dear?" his wife asked.

"Well, I was watching the bride's children throughout the ceremony, and they were far too cheerful to suit me."

Wills

There was a large gathering in the attorney's office to hear the reading of the will. The attorney announced, "This is one of the shortest wills you've ever heard."

Then, he lifted the paper before his eyes and read, "Being of sound mind, I spent every last cent before I died!"

Two widows were visiting together in a retirement center. One said, "My husband left me well fixed. I've got enough to live on the rest of my life."

"Well," the second one remarked, "my husband didn't do too well by me. In fact, he didn't even leave any insurance."

"You seem to be pretty well off," answered the first lady.

"I got the house and several other things, and I guess I've got enough to live on the rest of my life."

The first lady noticed a large diamond on her hand and remarked, "Where did you get the money to buy that gorgeous diamond ring?" she asked.

"Well, in his will he left a thousand dollars to buy a casket and a thousand dollars to buy the stone," she replied. "This," she said, pointing to the diamond ring, "is the stone!"

It's a man's world. When he's born, people ask, "How's the mother?"

When a man marries, people ask, "What did the bride wear?"

And when he dies, they ask, "How much did he leave her?"

For years, I pretended to love my rich aunt's cats so she would remember me in her will. It worked! When she died she left me the cats.

But it was different with my rich uncle. I found his doctor and thanked him for his treatment.

"You're not a patient of mine," the doctor replied.

"I know," I explained cheerfully, "but my uncle was, and I'm his heir!"

Actually, my uncle was quite successful before he died. His wife inherited three-hundred thousand dollars from the insurance company. She looked at the amount, sighed, and said to me, "I miss him so. Why, I'd give back fifty thousand dollars of this money to have him back."

Work (Business)

Question: What's the worst part of doing nothing?
Answer: You can't take the day off!

All the world's a stage and nobody wants to be a stagehand.

What a great country! People come here to make an honest living, and they hardly have any competition.

Dr. Quack advised his patient that the best thing that he could do was to get back to work immediately.

"Will that help my condition?" uttered the patient.

"Well, no," answered the doctor, "but at least you'll be able to pay me!"

The not-so-bright secretary complained, "I can't spell the words in the first place. How do you expect me to find them in the dictionary?"

Isn't it strange that work is something which when we have it we wish we didn't;

and when we don't we wish we did; and the object of most of it is to be able to afford not to do any of it?

My neighbor is lazy. He just sits in his easy chair. If his ship ever came in, he wouldn't bother to unload it.

Two women were talking over the back fence. "Shirley," one asked, "who do you reckon has the laziest husband, you or me?"

"I'd be afraid to say," the other replied, "but things are bad enough without starting a contest."

One woman said that her husband tried farming and gave it up because there were too many ups and downs. He had to wake up, then get up, wash up, chow down, and hitch up. Then when he checked up, he didn't have enough to pay down, so he just gave up.

Working makes me tired way up into next month. Besides, I need my beauty rest. Actually, I sleep well at nights and pretty well in the mornings, but in the afternoons I just toss and turn.

Times have changed. Forty years ago we worked twelve hours a day and it was called economic slavery. Today, we work fourteen hours a day and it's called moonlighting.

The younger generation doesn't seem to realize that getting up in the mornings is merely a matter of mind over mattress.

My grandson told me he couldn't brush his teeth because his batteries were dead!

Being a writer is not exactly a lucrative business. I heard of four men who died on the same day. One was a struggling author; he left his family five dollars; the second was a bookseller; he left fifty dollars. The third was a publisher; he left five-hundred dollars. the fourth was a dealer in waste paper; he left fifty thousand dollars.

Worry—(Nervousness)

Psychiatrist—A man who doesn't have to worry as long as others do.

Don't worry what others may think of you. They're probably not thinking of you anyway.

"Now, Jim," said the doctor, "as I have repeatedly told you after many thorough examinations, there is absolutely nothing wrong with your heart, so please stop worrying about it. If it will make you feel any better, I will personally guarantee you that your heart will last as long as you live!"

A pastor was walking the halls after Sunday School checking on how well his teachers had done in teaching the Sunday School lesson on the walls of Jericho that Sunday.

Little Billy was coming out of the class and the pastor walked up to him and asked, "Billy, why did the walls of Jericho come tumbling down?"

Of course, the pastor expected the young man to answer that the children of Israel were acting on faith in God's promises and they simply did what God asked them to do and the walls came tumbling down. However, little Billy had a different answer.

He replied, "Pastor, I didn't do it and I don't know who did."

Somewhat disappointed the pastor walked into the class to talk to Billy's teacher.

"I just asked Billy as he was leaving your class why the walls of Jericho came tumbling down, and he replied that he didn't do it. What kind of answer is that?"

The teacher replied, "Well, I've known Billy for a long time, Pastor, and if he said he didn't do it, then he didn't do it."

That afternoon, the pastor met with his deacons about the need for more effective teaching in his Sunday School.

"Deacons, I asked little Billy as he came out of his Sunday School class this morning why the walls of Jericho came tumbling down, and he replied that he didn't do it and he didn't know who did. I asked his Sunday School teacher to explain such an answer and the teacher replied, 'If Billy said he didn't do it, he didn't do it.'"

The chairman of the Deacons promptly interrupted the pastor and said, "This is a matter of grave concern to you, Pastor. Just let the Deacons take care of it. We'll write those Jericho people. If we owe them money, we'll send them money. If we need to send a crew down there to put the wall back up, we'll take care of it. Pastor, don't worry!"

When I speak before a group, I get as nervous as a mosquito at Fort Lauderdale's beach. I know what I'm there for; I just don't know where to start.

Have you heard about the convict who was eating his last supper before being executed. He ate everything on the platter except the Jello. When asked why, he explained, "No way! I'm not going to eat anything that's more nervous than I am!"

Did you hear about the kangaroo who complained to the doctor, "I don't know what's wrong with me lately. I don't feel jumpy"?

Worry is as useless as whispering in a boiler factory.

Ulcers result from mountain climbing over molehills.

> It's the little things that bother
> And put us on a rack;
> You can sit upon a mountain,
> But not upon a tack.

Sometimes I worry at night and can't go to sleep. Somebody told me to put a wastebasket beside my bed, and when I have trouble sleeping just pretend I'm throwing my worries in it. But it didn't work. Just about the time I was falling asleep the basket would overflow and I'd have to get up and empty it!

I used to worry about what people were thinking about me. Then I realized they weren't thinking about me at all. Instead, they were worrying about what other people were thinking of them.

Wrinkles

Most people don't mind the hands of time as much as the feet of crows.

Childhood: That time of life when you make funny faces in the mirror.
Middle age: That time of life when the mirror gets even.

All of those formulas for staying young will be totally unsuccessful until they learn how to iron out a few wrinkles.